## At Issue

# Piracy on the High Seas

# Other Books in the At Issue Series:

Affirmative Action

Animal Experimentation

Can Busy Teens Succeed Academically?

Can Celebrities Change the World?

Club Drugs

How Safe Is America's Infrastructure?

Nuclear Weapons

The Olympics

Polygamy

Teen Smoking

Teen Suicide

The U.S. Policy on Cuba

What Is the Future of the Music Industry?

What Is the Impact of E-Waste?

What Is the Impact of Tourism?

What Role Should the U.S. Play in the Middle East?

# At Issue

# Piracy on the High Seas

*Noah Berlatsky, Book Editor*

**GREENHAVEN PRESS**
*A part of Gale, Cengage Learning*

Detroit • New York • San Francisco • New Haven, Conn • Waterville, Maine • London

GALE
CENGAGE Learning·

Christine Nasso, *Publisher*
Elizabeth Des Chenes, *Managing Editor*

© 2010 Greenhaven Press, a part of Gale, Cengage Learning.

Gale and Greenhaven Press are registered trademarks used herein under license.

*For more information, contact:*
Greenhaven Press
27500 Drake Rd.
Farmington Hills, MI 48331-3535
Or you can visit our Internet site at gale.cengage.com

For product information and technology assistance, contact us at

Gale Customer Support, 1-800-877-4253
For permission to use material from this text or product, submit all requests online at www.cengage.com/permissions

Further permissions questions can be e-mailed to permissionrequest@cengage.com

Articles in Greenhaven Press anthologies are often edited for length to meet page requirements. In addition, original titles of these works are changed to clearly present the main thesis and to explicitly indicate the author's opinion. Every effort is made to ensure that Greenhaven Press accurately reflects the original intent of the authors. Every effort has been made to trace the owners of copyrighted material.

Cover image © Images.com/Corbis.

**LIBRARY OF CONGRESS CATALOGING-IN-PUBLICATION DATA**

Piracy on the high seas / Noah Berlatsky, book editor.
    p. cm. -- (At issue)
    Includes bibliographical references and index.
    ISBN 978-0-7377-4652-5 (hbk.) -- ISBN 978-0-7377-4653-2 (pbk.)
    1. Maritime terrorism--Juvenile literature. 2. Hijacking of ships--Juvenile literature. 3. Piracy--Juvenile literature. I. Berlatsky, Noah.
    HV6433.785.P57 2010
    364.16'4--dc22
                                                              2009037377

Printed in the United States of America
1 2 3 4 5 6 7 13 12 11 10 09

# Contents

Introduction     **7**

1. Southeast Asian Nations Must Coordinate     **10**
   Anti-Piracy Efforts
   *Catherine Zara Raymond*

2. Piracy in Southeast Asia Has Economic Causes     **20**
   *Adam J. Young*

3. Discreet U.S. Aid Is Vital to Fighting     **27**
   Piracy in Southeast Asia
   *Ian Storey*

4. Historical Piracy Provides Lessons for     **32**
   Dealing with Today's Somali Pirates
   *Virginia Lunsford*

5. The International Community Cannot     **44**
   Ignore Piracy in Somalia
   *Aidan Hartley*

6. Local Fleets Should Handle Somali Pirates     **50**
   *Peter Lehr*

7. The Indian Navy Should Engage Pirates     **54**
   Who Threaten Indian Nationals
   *Nitin Pai*

8. Military Courts Need to Be Established     **60**
   to Deal with Piracy
   *David B. Rivkin, Jr. and Lee A. Casey*

9. The U.S. Should Reconfigure Its Navy or     **65**
   Coast Guard to Deal with Piracy
   *Yoav Gortzak and Robert Farley*

10. To Fight Piracy at Sea, First Fight          71
    Lawlessness on Land
    *Rama Anom Kurniawan*

11. Somali "Pirates" Are Actually Trying to      75
    Stop Illegal Dumping and Fishing
    *Johann Hari*

12. Terrorists and Pirates Are Similar           80
    But Not the Same
    *Benerson Little*

13. States Can Do Little Against Maritime        85
    Terrorism and Piracy
    *William Langewiesche*

14. The Threat of Maritime Terrorism             95
    and Piracy Is Exaggerated
    *Sam Bateman*

Organizations to Contact                        108
Bibliography                                    114
Index                                           119

# Introduction

Pirates, as everyone knows, sailed long ago on wooden ships. They used a skull and crossbones emblem for a flag, taught their pet parrots to curse, and as often as not had wooden legs and hooks for hands. They said, "Arrr!" and "Avast me hearties!" and fought daringly with swords and pistols. If they captured you, they would force you to walk the plank, or, if you were lucky, they would maroon you on some distant island with a buried treasure chest. They were dangerous and evil, but also romantic and colorful, and were sometimes even noblemen in disguise.

This image of pirates is popular in fiction, from J.M. Barrie's *Peter Pan* to the more recent *Pirates of the Caribbean* movie series. Above all, we get our current ideas about pirates from Robert Louis Stevenson's 1883 novel *Treasure Island*. As David Cordingly wrote in *Under the Black Flag: The Romance and the Reality of Life Among the Pirates*, "The effect of *Treasure Island* on our perception of pirates cannot be overestimated. Stevenson linked pirates forever with maps, black schooners, tropical islands, and one-legged seamen with parrots on their shoulders," as well as with maps where an *X* showed the location of buried treasure.

A good deal of Stevenson's story, and of what we think of today when we think about pirates, is in fact true. The pirates Stevenson wrote about, who carried knives and old-fashioned guns and sailed in wooden ships, did actually exist. They were active between 1650 to 1725 during what is now known as the Golden Age of Piracy. These pirates were mostly from England and the English colonies, and they plundered shipping in the Atlantic and, especially, in the Caribbean.

Other aspects of Stevenson's pirates were based on truth as well. Pirates who sailed in tropical waters did, in reality, often pick up parrots as souvenirs and as valuables to sell once they got back to northern climes. Missing legs, limbs, and eyes were probably fairly common among pirate crews as well— pirates lived dangerous lives, and medical care was rudimentary, so injury could often result in amputation or the loss of an eye. Crippled sailors often served as the ship's cook. (Indeed, Stevenson's one-legged Long John Silver served as a cook, which is why a chain of restaurants is named after him.) And pirates really did sometimes maroon their victims. *Robinson Crusoe* was based on the experiences of Alexander Selkirk, a privateer (a semilegal pirate, authorized to attack foreign shipping by a government) who was marooned on a remote island for four years.

Other stories about pirates, though, have less basis in fact. Pirate speech, for example, is largely fanciful. Cecil Adams in his *Straight Dope* column of October 17, 2007, notes that "'Arrr' showed up late, probably in the movies of the 1930s ... much pirate lingo, like 'avast' was simply nautical speech of the time. ..." Pirate maps with X marking the spot and buried treasure were also fictional—pirates in general preferred to spend their treasure, not put it in a hole in the ground. The pirate flag, or "Jolly Roger," flown to frighten victims, was usually just plain black or red, with no skull and crossbones. In some situations, pirates would fly a false flag, pretending to be a ship from a friendly nation in order to lure victims closer.

Finally, one of the most famous of pirate cruelties, "walking the plank," seems to have been entirely made up. The one exception to this rule appears to have been Sadie the Goat, a pirate who Sara Lorimer discusses at some length in *Booty: Girl Pirates on the High Sea*. Sadie lived long after the Golden Age of Piracy; she terrorized New York's rivers and harbors in the 1860s. Lorimer notes that Sadie "read up on pirate lore," and, inspired by this research, made her captives walk the plank, not realizing (or perhaps not caring) that actual pirates preferred to simply shoot their victims.

Discussing Sadie brings up another important point about pirates: They did not disappear with the Golden Age. Piracy is simply robbery by sea, and it continues to this day.

Modern pirates are neither romantic nor old-fashioned. They often use motorboats and up-to-date weaponry: pistols, machine guns, or anything else they can get their hands on. Pirate attacks are especially common in areas where governments are weak and have trouble enforcing law and order. Thus, for several years in the late 1990s and early 2000s, the focus of pirate attacks was in the Strait of Malacca near Indonesia, which was experiencing civil unrest and a turbulent transition to democracy. As Indonesia's government stabilized, and thanks to a determined international effort, pirate attacks in the region fell so that "From January to late December 2007, we recorded zero percent pirate attacks in the Malacca Straits," according to an Indonesian defense official quoted by the AFP news agency on April 13, 2008.

As piracy has decreased in Indonesia, however, it has risen in the waters off the African state of Somalia. Somalia has experienced a long period of civil war, and its government is barely functional. As a result, pirates have been able to operate off its coasts with little interference. In April of 2009, a group of Somali pirates took over the U.S.-operated *Maersk Alabama*, the first time a U.S. ship had been seized by pirates in more than 200 years. Mark Mazzetti and Sharon Otterman, writing in *The New York Times* on April 8, 2009, noted that "An episode that at times seemed ripped from the pages of a Robert Louis Stevenson novel had its own 21st-century twists: the pirates conducted ransom negotiations using satellite telephones, and a United States Navy guided missile destroyer and other warships were sent to aid the hostages." The image of Golden Age Pirates will probably always linger, but pirates in Somalia and elsewhere seem set to remain a serious modern danger for some time to come.

# 1

# Southeast Asian Nations Must Coordinate Anti-Piracy Efforts

*Catherine Zara Raymond*

*Catherine Zara Raymond is an Associate Research Fellow at the Institute of Defence and Strategic Studies (IDSS), Nanyang Technological University, Singapore. She is a co-editor and contributing author of the volume* Best of Times, Worst of Times; Maritime Security in the Asia-Pacific. *She was previously an analyst at the Centre for the Study of Terrorism and Political Violence, University of St. Andrews, Scotland.*

*Piracy in Southeast Asia has increased due to economic factors and to U.S.-Soviet disengagement following the end of the Cold War. Piracy causes millions of dollars of losses and has the potential to cause environmentally devastating shipwrecks. Nations in Southeast Asia have implemented more patrols and are moving toward better coordination of anti-piracy efforts. These steps must be continued and expanded to reduce piracy in the region.*

The increase in the amount of commercial traffic traversing the region's waterways is another factor which accounts for the rise in incidence of piracy. Sea-borne trade has doubled every decade since 1945, and shipbuilding tonnage worldwide has doubled since 1990. This has substantially increased the number of potential targets for pirates to attack.

Another problem is the growing trend towards the use of 'skeleton crews', in other words ships staffed with the mini-

Catherine Zara Raymond, "Piracy in Southeast Asia: New Trends, Issues and Responses," *Harvard Asia Quarterly*, Fall 2005, pp. 8–13. Copyright © 2005 The President and Fellows of Harvard College. Reproduced by permission of author.

mum amount of people necessary. These crews are asked to carry out multiple tasks at the operational level and will find it difficult to perform anti-piracy security measures. Thus, ships are more easily boarded and taken over by the pirates.

## Effects of Piracy in the Region

Besides the obvious and increasing human toll, piracy is responsible for aggravating economic and financial damage to countries as well as the international shipping industry. Fraud, stolen cargoes, delayed trips, and increased insurance premiums are all consequences of piracy and have a direct economic effect on those at the receiving end of the crime. The impact of piracy is hard to gauge in monetary terms. Estimates of global piracy costs range from as low as US$250 million to US$16 billion a year. However, the frequency and fiscal damage of piracy is less than that of shore-based crimes in many countries in Southeast Asia; therefore there is a tendency to place piracy low on the list of law enforcement priorities. This is true particularly for Indonesia, whose defence and security resources are already stretched due to continued internal security problems and defence budget constraints. In addition, Indonesia benefits little from the trade that transits the Straits of Malacca. Unlike Singapore and Malaysia, it does not have a major port serviced by these pirate-infested waterways. The eastern coast of Sumatra, along which the Straits run, remains largely underdeveloped. For this reason, amongst others, Indonesia has traditionally lagged behind its neighbours when it comes to maritime security.

One final and perhaps often understated issue is the potential for a pirate attack to cause a major environmental disaster. In the Philip Channel, in the Singapore Straits, the interval between ships proceeding in any one direction is only approximately twenty minutes. During a pirate attack the crew is most often rounded up and held captive, and consequently unable to maintain look-out and other navigational responsibilities, which are essential when transiting the region's narrow waterways. The environmental consequences of a collision involving an unmanned oil tanker could be enormous.

Indeed, it is believed that an incident of this kind may have already taken place. In 1992, the Japanese super tanker the *Nagasaki Spirit* collided with the *Ocean Blessing*, which was zigzagging through shipping lanes at the northern end of the Straits of Malacca and possibly under pirate control. The accident and resulting fire killed all of the crew aboard *Ocean Blessing* and all but two of the tanker's crew. Fortunately, although 12,000 tons of oil spilled into the sea, because the oil was the light oil which evaporated, diffused, and disappeared rapidly in the tropical climate, major environmental damage was avoided.

## Coordinating an Anti-Piracy Response

As most piracy is legally considered armed robbery, any counter-measures are the responsibility of the state. The investigation, capture, prosecution and punishment of pirates who operate within territorial waters therefore varies due to the diverse national legal systems of the states in the region. However, given the transnational nature of piracy, multilateral cooperative measures are needed to effectively deal with the problem. Unfortunately, obstacles to cooperation are numerous. These may include concerns over the erosion of national sovereignty and differing political and economic priorities.

---

*The Trilateral Coordinated Patrols are also insufficient to reduce piracy. The main problem being that there is a lack of a provision for 'hot-pursuit' into each others' territorial waters.*

---

Despite these problems, the region witnessed the introduction of two new important maritime security measures in 2004. One was the International Ship and Port Facility Security Code (ISPS Code), which was created by the International Maritime Organisation [IMO] to introduce worldwide a range of new security requirements for vessels and port facilities. The other was the launch of the Trilateral Coordinated Patrol, which involved the navies of Malaysia, Indonesia and Singapore patrolling in a coordinated fashion in their respective territorial waters. Following the introduction of these two new measures in mid-2004, there was not, however, any significant reduction in the total number of incidents of piracy in the region in the second half of 2004. The figures for the first quarter of 2005 are more promising; for example, Indonesia only recorded 16 attacks as opposed to 21 over the same time period [in 2004]. However, this reduction is most probably a result of the devastation caused by the tsunami [of December 2004], which is likely to have either killed some of those involved in piracy or destroyed their boats and weapons, rather than because of any anti-piracy measures.

Although the ISPS Code significantly increases security awareness in the maritime industry, the standard of enforcement of the new IMO regulations varies from country to country. This is especially true in the case of states that have on their shipping registers flags of convenience vessels [ships for which the nationality of the owner is different from the country of registration.] These states 'lack the resources or people with sufficient expertise to enforce the standards that are acceptable to the shipping community at large'. In fact, in the majority of cases, one could argue that although security plans may be in place and security officers designated, the unfortunate reality is that it is often crewmembers of a fairly low rank and with limited training who are tasked to implement the Code.

The Trilateral Coordinated Patrols are also insufficient to reduce piracy. The main problem being that there is a lack of a provision for 'hot-pursuit' into each others' territorial waters. Although arrangements were put in place for communication to be established between the navies in the case of a cross-border chase to allow one navy to hand over to the other, they are unlikely to be as effective as the employment of 'hot-pursuit'.

More recently in 2005 a number of new measures have been or are in the process of being implemented in the region. In the latest development the littoral states [that is, countries bordering the waterway], with Thailand as an observer, [will] begin joint air patrols over the Malacca Strait in a bid to boost security in the waterway. The three states will each donate two planes for the patrols, which have been dubbed the 'Eye in the Sky' plan. It is hoped that the aerial patrols will provide a valuable supplement to the Trilateral Coordinated Patrols carried out by the navies of the littoral states. One significant advantage of the aerial patrols is that they will be able to fly for up to three nautical miles inside the territorial waters of the participating states, thus allowing for a reasonable 'transgression' of boundaries. In the sea-patrols the navies were limited to patrolling in their own territorial jurisdiction or on the high-seas.

On a less optimistic note, the 'Eye in the Sky' plan has already been criticized as being merely 'for show'. It is estimated that 70 sorties per week need to be carried out by the aerial patrols in order to effectively monitor the Strait 24/7. However, currently only 8 take place. There is also a lack of sea-patrol vessels available to carry out investigation and interdiction if necessary, following the sighting of a suspect vessel by the aerial patrols. Although the 'Eye in the Sky' plan clearly has room for significant improvement, the valuable deterrent effect it will have on potential attackers cannot be dismissed.

## Other Anti-Piracy Initiatives

Singapore, Japan, Laos and Cambodia became the first four states to formally adhere to the Regional Cooperation Agreement on Anti-Piracy (ReCAAP). Once six more participating states sign on, ReCAAP will enter into force and a new Information Sharing Centre will be set up in Singapore. The centre will facilitate communication and information exchanges between member countries and will improve the quality of statistics and reports on piracy and armed robbery against ships in the region.

Malaysia has recently announced a number of new maritime security initiatives. Armed police officers will now be placed on board selected tug boats and barges traversing the Malacca Strait. In addition, an escort service initiated in March [2005] will now be provided for vessels carrying valuable cargo in the Strait. In the same month Kuala Lumpur [Malaysia] also declared that it will start 24-hour radar surveillance of the Strait. Due to become operational in November [2005] is Malaysia's new Maritime Enforcement Agency. The new agency, made up of personnel from the navy, police and other government agencies, will be responsible for ensuring the security of the country's maritime zone against threats such as piracy and terrorism.

---

*Indonesia ... has initiated a multi-faceted approach to improving security. This includes programmes aimed at alleviating poverty and improving welfare.*

---

Singapore's new maritime security measures include the creation of Accompanying Sea Security Teams (ASSeT), which are tasked with boarding and escorting vessels singled out through shipping data analysis in order to detect and deter any criminal activity [aboard] these vessels and ensure that the threat is minimised. Singapore has just completed the installation of new radars at Changi Naval base to increase the radar coverage of its territorial waters. In addition it has increased navy and coast-guard patrols in its waters.

The Singaporean and Indonesian navies have launched a system that provides real-time radar surveillance for the Singapore Strait. The new system, known as SURPIC, or the 'Surface Picture, Surveillance System', will be located on Batam Island in Indonesia.

Although still at the discussion level, Malaysia, Indonesia and the Philippines are considering allowing their naval forces to pursue pirates into each other's waters. If implemented, this new agreement would be an unprecedented step in the fight against piracy.

Finally, Indonesia, traditionally the weakest link in terms of maritime security in the region, has initiated a multi-faceted approach to improving security. This includes programmes aimed at alleviating poverty and improving welfare, in particular in those remote areas which border the Straits of Malacca and Singapore, and increasing local people's awareness of laws and regulations and strengthening sanctioning institutions. It also announced that its navy plans to buy up to 60 modern patrol vessels over the next decade in order to strengthen maritime security in its waters.

These new measures, if successfully implemented, should significantly improve security in the region's waterways [as] they display a greater level of regional cooperation than seen previously. The implementation of ReCAAP and Indonesia's internal development programmes is also a welcome move away from the tendency to focus countermeasures on tackling the problem solely at sea.

---

*Cooperation between the region's states must be enhanced to include agreements on 'hot-pursuit' and more mechanisms for intelligence sharing.*

---

In the meantime, however, pirate attacks will continue in the region's waterways, and ship owners are increasingly looking elsewhere for ways to enhance their security. One solution that has rapidly gained popularity in recent months is the employment of private security companies who are offering armed escort services through the Straits. For between US$10,000 and US$100,000 a shipping company can have armed Gurkhas [people from Nepal and Northern India] escort vessels and helicopter scouts securing its [ships'] passage through the Straits. Despite assurances that the escorts merely act as a deterrent to potential attackers, they have provoked a strong response from the littoral states. Both Indonesia and Malaysia have declared that these companies should not provide armed escorts through their waters. Malaysia even announced its plans to detain ships with private armed escorts. However, the Malaysian Defence Minister subsequently stated that armed escorts would be allowed to pass though Malaysia's stretch of the Malacca Strait, provided that their passage is continuous and expeditious.

## More Must Be Done to Fight Piracy

Piracy in Southeast Asia is likely to remain a major security concern for governments and the shipping industry for some years to come. It also acts as a constant reminder of the potential ease with which terrorists could use similar tactics to carry out an attack. As long as piracy continues, it clearly illustrates that a certain amount of anarchy or lawlessness prevails in the region's waterways. Piracy levels are therefore an indicator of the overall security in the region.

America's war on terrorism following 9/11 put maritime security under the spotlight and prompted the region's states to begin improving maritime security. This assertive posture must be maintained. Cooperation between the region's states must be enhanced to include agreements on 'hot-pursuit' and more mechanisms for intelligence sharing.

In the Straits of Malacca the need to address the problem of piracy has just become even more urgent. Following a risk assessment of the area, the Joint War Committee (JWC) of Lloyd's Market Association declared the Straits a 'high-risk zone' and added [the place] to its list of areas which are at risk to war, strikes, terrorism and related perils. Others on the list are countries such as Iraq, Somalia and Lebanon. Indonesian ports along the Straits were also added to the list.

This move by the JWC could result in higher insurance premiums for the ships that transit the Straits or call at some Indonesian ports. When war risk premiums were applied to the Yemeni port of Aden, container shipping lines were forced to divert to neighbouring ports. The resulting impact on the Yemeni economy was severe.

---

*Long-term solutions need to be found to address the root causes of piracy, which include poor socio-economic conditions.*

---

Major users of the region's waterways must begin to accept a greater responsibility for enhancing maritime security. Japan is one user state that has contributed significantly to efforts to improve safety and security in the Straits of Malacca. For example, it is currently providing support to Indonesia in order to help it implement the ISPS Code in its ports. Japan's efforts could be used as a model for other states wishing to provide assistance—in particular in the areas of maritime enforcement capacity building, personnel training and resources—in the future.

It would be advantageous if all the Southeast Asian states signed the IMO's 1988 Convention on the Suppression of Unlawful Acts [SUA] against the Safety of Maritime Navigation: 'Ratification of the convention gives signatory governments the power to prosecute people caught in their own territorial waters for acts of piracy committed under another country's jurisdiction.' Although the SUA Convention has been signed by 126 out of 166 IMO Member states, which is a high number of contracting states in comparison to many other maritime conventions, a number of countries are conspicuously missing from the list, given their important position as guardians of strategically important waterways. In Southeast Asia, only Singapore, Vietnam, Philippines, Myanmar and Brunei are signatories to this convention. ReCAAP should also be signed by those regional states that have not yet done so.

Finally, long-term solutions need to be found to address the root causes of piracy, which include poor socio-economic conditions. Indonesia's efforts in this area are a step in the right direction but more will need to be done in the near future, if the problem of piracy in Southeast Asia is to be resolved.

# 2

# Piracy in Southeast Asia Has Economic Causes

*Adam J. Young*

*Adam J. Young is a scholar whose work has focused on Southeast Asian piracy and conflict transformation. He was affiliated with the East-West Center in Honolulu, and now works for a non-profit mediation organization.*

*Southeast Asia has developed rapidly over the last thirty years. This has led to greater inequality and to dislocation as people move in search of better wages. Development has also increased shipping. In addition the region is home to a large subsistence population that makes its living from fishing, which has been hard hit by environmental change and depletion of fish stocks. Economic problems were exacerbated by the Asian economic crisis of 1997. All these factors together mean that there are many very poor people in the region who have the incentive and the opportunity to plunder shipping.*

Over the last thirty years the processes of globalization have stimulated widespread economic growth throughout Southeast and East-Asia, leading to a rapid pace of development. When measured in terms of gross domestic product (GDP) and the standard measures of industrial output, as well as standard markers of human conditions like literacy, infant mortality rates, and life expectancy, Southeast Asia has made impressive progress since the 1960s. . . . Overall, real strides have been made in reducing poverty and generally increasing the material standard of life for people in many parts of Southeast Asia. However, the rapid economic development of the last thirty years has been uneven, and has had unintended, negative consequences that are important for understanding why piracy has resurfaced as a significant threat in the region.

One of the primary problems is that political development in the region has not kept pace with economic development. Despite unprecedented growth and the very real material gains that have been made, there are still large portions of populations that have either been left behind without access to economic opportunity, or have become unwitting victims of the rapid economic development, including many groups of maritime-oriented peoples. Historic social networks are breaking down as traditional economic and social systems give way and adapt to the pace of modernization. Many regional governments are unwilling or unable to help those who are being left behind. Factories are attracting thousands of young people from villages to pursue more viable livelihoods and, while many continue to financially support their families, their absence is a missing link in the traditional social security network. This [change,] combined with an almost complete lack of institutionalized social security[,] has left many facing new survival challenges.

## Economic Growth Fuels Piracy

The negative aspects of economic development and globalization have stimulated massive dislocation of populations, as millions of people move in search of better wages, even moving across international boundaries. This development has provided opportunities for legitimate employment. However, it has also led to rising incidences of poverty, creating a labour pool for criminal activities like prostitution, drugs, [and] petty extortion rackets, among many others, and when the right seafaring skills are available, possibly piracy. These problems which have manifested themselves during years of economic growth suggest weak state development, or simply economic development that has outpaced the capacity of the state to redistribute the profits effectively.

Economic growth in the region, especially East Asia, has translated into heavy increases in sea traffic through Southeast Asia, stimulating maritime economies but also creating new regulatory problems. . . . More than 50,000 ships annually transit these waters, [counting] only . . . large freighters and tankers. Furthermore, total numbers of tonnage during 2000 were expected to rise 9.2 per cent, and twenty-foot container equivalents (TEUs) were expected to climb 6.8 per cent, largely due to the expanding Chinese economy, with overall world trade expected to have risen 8.5 per cent despite rising oil prices, which means increasing traffic through the pirate-infested waters of maritime Southeast Asia. Not only does this mean more ships to track, and a greater number of potential targets for pirates, but it also means that there will be more crews to try [to] track as well.

Seafarers numbering 1.2 million, or half the world merchant fleet, sail under flags of convenience, which means "ships can be owned by nationals of one country and be registered in another," and most "major ship-owning nations sail under flags of convenience," providing registration for boats and crews as a business. Flags of convenience problematize the tracking of true identities of crew and ships, but they offer seafarers the opportunity to make wages far higher than under their own national flags. Therefore it is not in their interest to question ownership of the boat or the identities of the crew, and therefore screening processes are minimal. Lax enforcement of regulations is compounded by relatively easy access to forged documents, as pirates have been caught with passports from multiple countries, making their identification difficult. In 2001 alone the International Maritime Organization (IMO) reported 13,000 cases of falsified documents among various ships crew, most of which were from Indonesia and the Philippines. This provides easy opportunities for insiders to be planted who can relay boat position, crew complement, and/or ship layout to attackers.

## Maritime Poverty Fuels Piracy

A significant portion of the total population of Southeast Asia lives near the coast and [is] dependent on the seas for . . . food and livelihoods. For example, in 1998 in the Philippines approximately one million people were employed in fishing, or approximately 5 per cent of the work force, of which only 57,000 were employed on large vessels, implying the rest were small-scale fishermen. In Indonesia at the same time, there were approximately 4.6 million people employed in fishing, or approximately 4 per cent of the population if their families are included. These figures represent only those reported to the government, and likely there are millions more people who earn some part of their living from the seas that do not report to the government. . . . These numbers also do not include the tens of thousands of small traders and merchants who ply these waters.

*"Some of these ships can feed a whole Indonesian village. And these guys have nothing to lose."*

In both trades, even under ideal circumstances, individual operators without substantial personal capital are often at the margins of poverty, making enough to repay debt and provide the essentials of survival, but little else. Like their poor counterparts on land who have little money for capital improvements or to buy more land to farm, maritime peoples maintain a tenuous balance of sustainable survival, especially as they often find themselves in some of the poorest regions of Southeast Asia and isolated from major economic centres.

Fishing catches can be fickle, depending on either unpredictable or uncontrollable variables like the weather, and fluctuations in the local and international markets can be potentially disastrous. In the contemporary world, fisher folk are also beset by massive illegal fishing operations (which many poor folks also engage in) that use dynamiting techniques or worse, destroying reefs, fish habitat, and maritime people's future livelihood. There is also massive illegal fishing in the form of unregistered foreign vessels who "pirate" the waters for increasingly rare fish. Rapid economic growth has severely damaged much of the environment on which many depend for their livelihoods, either through over-exploitation or pollution. As catches decline across the region, competition for what is left increases. Facing these challenges, maritime peoples are generally the poorest of the poor, having to eke out a living from finicky resources that are frequently under attack, and the possibility of bringing home the equivalent of a year's income, or more in one raid must prove an irresistible temptation to some. For example, Thai fishermen who traditionally operated in the Gulf of Thailand began to seriously deplete fish stocks by the 1970s, and moved out into other nations' waters, or were forced to find other sources of income, such as preying on Vietnamese boat people. As one representative of a shipping company said, "Some of these ships can feed a whole Indonesian village. And these guys have nothing to lose."

---

*Markets tumbled so quickly that responses were too slow in coming to stave off disaster for many states.*

---

## The Asian Economic Crisis Fueled Piracy

The Asian economic crisis of 1997 exacerbated the problems that had developed during times of relative prosperity: the inequalities of rapid economic development, the resulting marginalization and dislocation of people, the expansion of organized criminal networks. Over all aspects of weak state development, and the resurgence of piracy. Even though some authors have convincingly argued that Southeast Asians have weathered the economic crisis better than some of the direst predictions [suggested they might], there [were] unarguably considerable effects, which stimulated piracy.

One of the most destructive aspects of the crisis was the rapidity with which it seized the region. The linked markets and interconnected economic structures forged through processes of globalization, and built upon questionable political and economic policy, created a monetary ripple in Thailand that quickly grew into a tsunami that inundated the region. Markets tumbled so quickly that responses were too slow in coming to stave off disaster for many states. Indonesia in particular was hard hit with massive unemployment, consumer price indices jumped to as high as 77 per cent, leading to high expenditures on daily necessities [such as] food (up to 62 per cent of income in 1999), and approximately 18 per cent of people lived below the poverty line. Many of these statistics have improved in the last couple of years, but between 1997 and 1999 the general welfare of Indonesian people as a result of the economic crisis was deeply affected. In the Philippines despite growing national income and savings levels, poverty and unemployment are also on the rise, particularly in those regions where piracy and smuggling have emerged as major problems, such as the southern Philippines and the Autonomous Region of Muslim Mindanao (ARMM), including Jolo and Tawi Tawi in the Sulu Sea.

While the economic crisis was instrumental in the recent upsurge in piracy of the last five to six years, piracy numbers had begun to climb in the 1970s, 80s, and 90s, starting in 1975 [after] the end of the Vietnam Conflict, and continuing through the 1980s, with hundreds of attacks on Vietnamese refugees ("boat people") in the Gulf of Thailand and around Hong Kong, as well as a surge of incidents in the Sulu region.

These trends began during some of the biggest boom years in Southeast Asia. Uneven, rapid economic development without commensurate political development to control the expanding economies created the foundations of poverty, which in part stimulated the rise of piracy, and the economic crisis only made existing conditions worse.

# 3

# Discreet U.S. Aid Is Vital to Fighting Piracy in Southeast Asia

*Ian Storey*

*Ian Storey is a fellow at the Institute of Southeast Asian Studies.*

*Piracy has been much reduced in Southeast Asia between 2004 and 2009. In part, greater regional coordination has been a cause, as have actions by the Indonesian government. Also important has been low-key aid from the United States in the forms of money and equipment. Despite these successes, the global economic crash may fuel more piracy, so continued vigilance is necessary.*

According to the International Maritime Bureau's (IMB) annual report released last week, 65 attacks took place in regional waters last year [2008] compared with a high of 187 in 2003.

In the Strait of Malacca, the vital strategic waterway that links North-east Asia and the western Pacific with the Indian Ocean and used by more than 100,000 local and international vessels each year, the number of reported incidents fell to just two, down from 34 in 2004 (though the number of attacks in the Singapore Strait doubled from three to six between 2007 and [2008]).

Particularly striking has been the improved security situation in Indonesian waters, the locus of the piracy and sea rob-

Ian Storey, "What's Behind Dramatic Drop in S-E Asian Piracy," *The Straits Times*, January 19, 2009. Reproduced by permission.

bery problem in South-east Asia. Only 28 attacks took place in Indonesian ports and territorial waters last year [2008], compared to 121 in 2003.

The greatly improved law and order situation in South-east Asian waters stands in sharp contrast to the deteriorating situation in Africa. Last year, the IMB recorded 189 attacks on the continent, 111 committed by well-organised pirate gangs operating in the Gulf of Aden and off the coast of Somalia, including 42 hijackings and the kidnapping for ransom of 815 sailors.

## Why Has Piracy Been Reduced?

What explains the dramatic decrease in acts of maritime crime in South-east Asia?

Improved security cooperation among Singapore, Indonesia and Malaysia has been one key element. In mid-2004, against the backdrop of international and especially US clamour to stem the tide of rising piracy attacks in the Strait of Malacca, the three nations launched year-round coordinated naval patrols known as the Malacca Strait Patrols (MSP). In 2005, combined air patrols were added to the MSP.

The trilateral initiative has not only resulted in the arrest of maritime marauders, but also acted as a strong deterrent to other would-be pirates. Late last year, the MSP was given a further boost when Thailand agreed to participate.

Of equal if not greater importance [have] been the actions of the Indonesian government to address the problem. In 2005, President Susilo Bambang Yudhoyono ordered his navy to increase patrols in the country's waters adjacent to the Malacca Strait and to step up intelligence-gathering operations in fishing communities along the Sumatran coast and around the Riau Islands in an effort to round up maritime criminals. The IMB applauded Indonesia in its 2008 annual report for its 'tireless efforts in curbing piracy and armed robbery in its waters.'

Assistance provided by external powers has also been instrumental in containing the piracy problem. While regional countries, especially Indonesia and Malaysia, have rejected the idea of foreign navies patrolling South-east Asian waters, they have welcomed support from external powers in the form of capacity building: training programmes, joint exercises, equipment transfer and information exchange.

## The U.S. Provides Anti-Piracy Aid

Among all of South-east Asia's security partners, the United States has taken the lead role in capacity-building efforts. In 2006, US legislation authorised the Pentagon to [help] foreign countries improve maritime security and counter-terrorism operations under the Global Train and Equip Programme (also known as Section 1206 authorisation). Indonesia, Malaysia and the Philippines have been among the prime beneficiaries of the programme.

---

*Due to the global financial crisis, Jakarta has slashed the country's already modest defence budget by 15 per cent for 2009.*

---

In 2007–2008, the US provided Indonesia with US$47.1 million worth of equipment to improve its maritime situational awareness capabilities, including five coastal surveillance radars installed along the Indonesian side of the Malacca Strait and seven more along the Makassar Strait and in the Celebes Sea.

During the same period, Malaysia received US$16.3 million in Section 1206 funding, including US$13.6 million for nine coastal radar stations along the Sabah coast and US$2.2 million to improve aerial surveillance along the Malacca Strait. Since 2006, the Philippines has received US$15.5 million to upgrade its maritime surveillance interdiction capabilities.

For 2008–2009, the Pentagon is seeking an additional US$9.5 million under Section 1206 funding for coastal radars to be sited in the Sulu archipelago and US$3.5 million for additional radar facilities for Indonesia.

While some of the US funding has gone towards improving security in the Strait of Malacca, most has been spent on projects in the Sulu and Celebes seas, also known as the triborder sea area. The triborder area has long been neglected by the governments of Indonesia and the Philippines, becoming a haven for illegal maritime activities such as piracy and trafficking in narcotics, guns and people. More worryingly, the triborder area has also been utilised by terrorists belonging to the Abu Sayyaf Group and Jemaah Islamiyah as a means of moving among the southern Philippines, Sabah and Indonesia.

In order to avoid domestic sensitivities, US assistance to the three countries has been low-key. All of the equipment that has been provided is manned and operated by the host nation. In assessing the effectiveness of the aid, one Pentagon agency, the Defence Security and Cooperation Agency, has described the Global Train and Equip Programme to be 'the single most important tool to shape the environment of counter terrorism outside of Iraq and Afghanistan.'

## Anti-Piracy Efforts Must Continue

Despite the considerable gains made in improving security in South-east Asia's maritime domains over the past four years, regional countries can ill-afford to let down their collective guard. The IMB has repeatedly cautioned against complacency and the need to sustain initiatives such as the MSP. The most important participant in the MSP, Indonesia, is at particular risk of 'patrol fatigue' because the MSP consumes a high proportion of the navy's limited resources, especially ships, fuel and manpower.

Due to the global financial crisis, Jakarta[, Indonesia,] has slashed the country's already modest defence budget by 15 per cent for 2009. Worryingly, both the Indonesian and Malaysian navies have warned that incidents of piracy in South-east Asia may experience an upsurge this year due to deteriorating socio-economic conditions—one of the primary causes of piracy—associated with the global financial downturn. Continued vigilance is therefore paramount.

# 4

# Historical Piracy Provides Lessons for Dealing with Today's Somali Pirates

*Virginia Lunsford*

*Virginia Lunsford is an associate professor of history at the U.S. Naval Academy who specializes in maritime and European history. She is the author of* Piracy and Privateering in the Golden Age Netherlands.

*Piracy of the past can teach us about piracy of today. That is why studying the Barbary corsairs who plundered Western vessels off the coast of North Africa between 1500 and 1832 has value. The corsairs were successful because there was a large refugee population to draw manpower from, because they had the support of many port cities and of the Ottoman Empire, and because they were united by a shared Muslim identity. European naval power was therefore unable to eradicate them for 300 years. The lesson for dealing with pirates today is that naval power is not enough; instead, governments must attack the organizational structures, state sponsorship, and political/economic turmoil that make piracy possible.*

The Golden Age of Piracy—from approximately 1570 to around 1730—was an era when robbery on the high seas was widespread, lucrative, and threatening. Although nowadays it has been romanticized in such films as Disney's *Pirates of the Caribbean* trilogy, piracy back then was actually violent,

Virginia Lunsford, "What Makes Piracy Work?" Reprinted from *Proceedings Magazine*, December 2008, with permission. Copyright © 2008 U.S. Naval Institute/www.usni.org.

frightening, destabilizing, and thoroughly illegitimate, at least from the point of view of governing authorities. Its history provides a variety of case studies and models that illustrate how these groups operated and to what degree their activities continued, despite opposition and military confrontation.

In turn, these models offer ways to analyze the pirates of the contemporary world—including those now operating off the coasts of Africa—so we can ascertain their viability and learn how to combat them. Ultimately, case studies reveal that long-term, intractable, flourishing piracy is a complex activity that relies on five integral factors: an available population of potential recruits, a secure base of operations, a sophisticated organization, some degree of outside support, and cultural bonds that engender vibrant group solidarity. Activities that interfere with the smooth workings of any of these factors weaken piracy's sustainability.

## The Barbary Pirates Terrorized North Africa

From about 1500 to 1832, the Barbary corsairs of North Africa made the Mediterranean a highly dangerous place, regularly attacking and plundering Western trading vessels. Their ineradicable presence, frightening success, and savage violence over three long centuries stemmed directly from their exploitation of the aforementioned five fundamental qualities. Europeans were terrified of these marauders, for the North Africans zealously pursued and looted any and all Western ships, no matter their nationality.

Religious ideology characterized and permeated this conflict, with each side—the North Africans and the Europeans (and later Americans), respectively—citing their Muslim and Christian identities as the primary reason they were locked in a state of opposition. While the loss of trade goods was bad enough, what most terrified the Europeans was that the corsairs routinely seized sailors and passengers from Western ships, using them as slave labor on board corsair ships or in their sponsoring cities, collecting ransoms from their faraway kinsmen and countrymen, or selling them in the slave markets of North Africa and Turkey. People were the corsairs' primary targets. Ships and property were beneficial, but they were secondary objectives.

The corsairs were based in several large North African port cities, including Algiers, Tunis, Tripoli, and Sal and Mamora (later Morocco). While nominally controlled by the Ottoman Empire, the denizens of these settlements were actually granted wide latitude from the Sultan to behave as they wished. The corsairs' origins lay in the Spanish Catholic evictions of Muslims from the Iberian Peninsula (circa 1300–1500), which had created a population of embittered refugees in the North African cities and instigated the early 16th-century Spanish invasions of North Africa.

Lacking a naval response to repel the Spanish aggressors, each of the port cities adopted Ottoman naval technology, combat techniques, shipboard operations, and raiding strategies, and accepted Ottoman financial support, all in exchange for a loose allegiance to the empire.

The resulting arrangement was a win-win situation for both the Turks and the North Africans. The port cities now had the means to combat the aggressive Spanish, and the Ottomans were happy to have a naval bulwark along the southern Mediterranean coast, thereby impeding European endeavors to control the sea.

## Barbary Piracy Throve on Muslim/Christian Conflict

Since these events followed closely on the heels of and indeed were inextricably entwined with the tensions stemming from the Crusades and European Reconquest of the Iberian Peninsula, the confrontations that ensued were articulated in the ideological idiom of religious conflict: Muslims versus Christians. At the same time, however, a less obvious but no less important reason for the clash stemmed from the shift in trade patterns from the Mediterranean to the Atlantic and Indian oceans, a change that deprived North African port economies of commercial activity.

*In keeping with their ideological perspective [as] victims of religious persecution and attempted invasion, the corsairs did not see their actions as piratical in the least.*

Each port city sponsored and sheltered its own fleet of corsairs, pledging financial support and rewards, political protection, and physical refuge. Accordingly, corsairs brought their captured goods, ships, and prisoners to their respective sponsoring city. It was a symbiotic relationship that worked well for the duration of the phenomenon, ensuring the corsairs protection and their city's economic survival.

Over the course of the 16th century, following the Ottoman naval model they had adopted, the corsairs used galleys commanded by local North Africans and rowed by slaves. As the 17th century unfolded, however, they also acquired European sailing ships and began to include an increasing number of dispossessed European sailors in their crews. Many of these so-called renegade Westerners ended up occupying the highest positions in the chain of command and had extremely successful careers as North African raiders.

In keeping with their ideological perspective [as] victims of religious persecution and attempted invasion, the corsairs did not see their actions as piratical in the least. On the contrary, they believed themselves to be revered warriors whose raiding activities defended their people and their faith and the economic sustenance and military security of their home ports. The West, however, condemned the corsairs as pirates, for their marauding did not at all conform to European rules of engagement or stipulations for legal commerce raiding.

As the raiding intensified over the years, the corsairs' hunting grounds expanded. While they always represented a grave threat to Mediterranean shipping, their attacks were by no means confined there, especially after they acquired the means and equipment to operate European-style sailing ships. Rather, in their quest for Christian quarry, the corsairs regularly prowled the Canary Islands and the African coast, even going as far as the Red Sea region. They also ventured into European waters, cruising along the coasts of Portugal, Spain, and France, and into the northern seas as well, making their way into the waters surrounding the Netherlands, England, and even around Iceland, which they raided spectacularly on at least one occasion.

After the mid-17th century, the corsairs increasingly took to the seas in large, powerful fleets, each including at least 20 vessels. They attacked ships and coastal settlements, and everywhere they went, the goal was still the same: hunt down Western goods and kidnap Western people.

---

*The corsairs captured and enslaved tens of thousands of Christian men, women, and children.*

---

The Barbary corsairs became infamous for their reputed violence. Regardless of how savage they really were, the perception among early-modern Europeans was that the North Africans were uncivilized and ruthless. Some modern scholars argue that accusations made against the corsairs were borne more out of fear and prejudice than actual circumstances. Moreover, it is important to remember that many practices, which in our eyes are shocking examples of cruel and unusual punishment, were by early-modern standards quite normal; all early-modern states—including those of Europe—employed harsh means of corporal and capital punishment.

But the stories are still sobering. Allegedly first-hand accounts written by witnesses and survivors of Barbary captivity describe dreadful places where thousands of pitiful Christian slaves (in 1621, supposedly more than 32,000 in Algiers alone) were, among other things, tortured, worked harshly and ceaselessly; and housed in dark, hot, vermin-infested prisons, where lice and fleas ate at their skin. North African youths jeered and threw stones, urine, and feces at them and burned them alive.

Methods of torture included bludgeonings, setting feet and hair afire, public whippings, impaling on pikes and giant hooks, genital mutilation, burial alive, and even crucifixion. Over the course of their existence, the corsairs captured and enslaved tens of thousands of Christian men, women, and children. Those who were not ransomed successfully could be worked to death and then denied the decency of a proper burial. Instead, early-modern sources decried, their corpses were left to rot and be eaten by dogs. Together these texts provide vivid anecdotes testifying to the corsairs' cruelty and rapaciousness [plundering].

## Europe Responded to Piracy

How did Europeans deal with the scourge of the Barbary corsairs? First, enormous effort went into liberating European captives through the payment of ransoms. To this end, liberation societies were born, associations whose sole purpose was to collect funds for the deliverance of Western slaves. In addition, many states and communities imposed a "Turk's rate" tax as a means to amass money for slaves' emancipation. Finally, Western governments sometimes presented the North Africans with gifts and/or monetary remuneration to expedite the process. Officially designated agents drawn from an extensive network of Catholic orders and Jewish merchants acted as middlemen and took the collected funds to North Africa to purchase slaves' freedom.

Second, European governments negotiated diplomatic agreements with the various North African city-states, and even the Ottoman Sultan himself. These treaties were typically uncoordinated efforts, meaning that they represented an agreement solely between one Western nation and one North African settlement. They often involved the payment of special sums of protection money to the sponsoring North African cities, thus avoiding Barbary harassment. (This was a technique employed especially by Western nations that lacked a strong naval presence in the Mediterranean.) Frequent expirations and changeable terms necessitated a constant revisiting of these diplomatic accords. Overall, the efficacy of the treaties ebbed and flowed over the years.

---

*The North African corsairs were effectively organized. . . .*
*They were sheltered by secure bases of operations. . . .*
*And among themselves they were animated by sturdy*
*bonds of ideological solidarity.*

---

Third, Western navies also patrolled the waters to stamp out the corsair nuisance. Sometimes, these naval forays resulted in concentrated attacks against a particular North African port city, or demonstrations of naval might in a city's harbor to intimidate the city leadership and encourage the release of slaves. Naval missions departed regularly and enjoyed some success, capturing Barbary raiders and either executing them or selling them into slavery. Such fleets typically cruised the Spanish and Portuguese coasts and Mediterranean Sea. If they apprehended a corsair vessel, they liberated any captive Christians, confiscated the weapons, auctioned the goods at the nearest friendly port, and took the enemy crew prisoner for later strategic disposal.

Western governments also pledged handsome rewards to any of their ships that seized a Barbary vessel. Special incentives included bonus wages, equal access to profits earned from the sale of the ship's goods, and for the captain of each conquering naval vessel the right to take the ship's provisions and small weaponry.

Fourth, European trading nations enacted protocols to protect their shipping against Barbary harassment. Directives from the 17th-century Netherlands, for example, included instructions to ship owners regarding the minimum size of vessels, type and quantity of weapons, and size of crews. Dutch ships were also required to convoy with at least one other similar vessel and were forbidden to transport any ordnance or naval stores to North African cities. Guilty parties were punished with severe fines and even execution. To detect any recalcitrant ship owners, the government developed an inspection system using the local magistrates of the relevant ports. It also created incentives for these local authorities (as well as for fellow mariners) to report ships not in compliance with the rules.

## Europe Could Not Defeat the Pirates for 300 Years

To a degree, these solutions saved Western lives. Still, though, they did not directly undermine any of the five fundamental factors accounting for corsair potency and durability. Consquently, the Barbary menace was impossible to eradicate for some 300 years. Why?

The North African corsairs were effectively organized following Ottoman naval tradition. They were sheltered by secure bases of operations in the form of the North African ports and economically and politically supported by both their sponsoring cities and ultimately, the Ottoman Sultan. And among themselves they were animated by sturdy bonds of ideological solidarity. Even the European renegades converted to Islam.

The West finally suppressed the corsairs, but not until the early decades of the 1800s when they were in a less vigorous state. In a series of confrontations, Western navies were able to forge (sometimes coerce) diplomatic treaties (e.g., the 1796 agreement with the independent Morocco). They also fought the corsairs and their North African sponsors in wars (e.g., the 1801–05 war between Tripoli and the fledging United States, whence comes the reference to the "shores of Tripoli" in *The Marines' Hymn*). And finally, they were able to vanquish sponsoring cities (e.g., the 1830 French invasion of Algiers, which signaled the definitive end of the Barbary corsairs). All of these Western triumphs were predicated on the use of sufficiently strong navies. But naval power alone did not do the trick.

In addition to navies, other forces were at work and created favorable conditions for Western success. Compared to the glory days of the 17th century, the Ottoman Empire was weaker economically and politically and thus less interested in corsair activities. Its bonds with the North African ports were even more tenuous, if they existed at all. For their part, the North African city-states were less supportive of corsair activities and less impervious to attack than they had been.

Furthermore, with refugees from the Iberian Peninsula long since absorbed and the absence of a steady pool of Western renegades, it was no longer as easy demographically to outfit a fleet of corsair ships. Among the corsairs themselves, ideological motivations still had their power, but less so. Therefore, the corsairs were less passionate about their enterprise and less willing to risk all. By the 19th century, then, superior Western navies were dealing with a weaker phenomenon, and so strong naval action could result in decisive victory.

## Lessons for Dealing with Piracy Today

As the rest of the world considers what to do about the increasingly problematic modern Somali pirates, it would behoove us to think beyond superficial and simple naval solutions on the high seas and consider the five factors underlying the long and productive careers of the Mediterranean corsairs.

To analyze Somali piracy more deeply and ultimately suppress it, we must ask ourselves these vital questions:

- Who are these Somali pirates?

- Where do they find recruits, and how many of them are available?

- Why do they take up piratical activities?

- Do we know the exact number, character, and location of all of their havens?

- Are these pirates organized, and if so, how are they organized, and is this organization strong and effective?

- Do the Somali pirates enjoy any outside sources of support? States or groups (including terrorist groups) that are providing money, goods, weapons, intelligence, or other help to their cause?

- Do these pirates maintain close bonds between one another with a keen sense of solidarity and cohesion, and if so, what is the nature of this solidarity, from where does it come, and is it powerful and abiding?

---

*The key to eradicating Somali piracy lies in interrupting the larger, complex system that supports it.*

---

We know some of the preliminary answers to these questions from intelligence gathered by American agencies. Today's Somali pirates are, in general, trained militia fighters based in the semi-autonomous regions of Puntland and Somaliland. They do not call themselves pirates. Organizationally, the piracy is based on the clan system so influential in Somalia. But it is allegedly controlled by elements within the Somali government as well as businessmen in Puntland.

The pirates are based in camps located adjacent to coastal port villages, and they also deploy previously captured ships as sea-going bases, or mother-ships. We do not know how intense the bonds of solidarity are among these raiders, but one would guess that relations are strong since the piracy overlays the indigenous clan system. At this time, analysts discern few clear links to terrorism, but this possible development is of ongoing concern.

---

*One of the vital lessons the history of the golden age of piracy imparts is that pirates can do serious damage with what seem to be unformidable naval assets.*

---

The key to eradicating Somali piracy lies in interrupting the larger, complex system that supports it. It is essential that the pirates be intercepted in action on the high seas, and the United States and its allies should continue to meet this objective. However, the situation is more complicated than that, and the longer the system is permitted to stay in place and grow, the more intractable the piracy problem will become.

Possible courses of action include somehow interrupting the flow of recruits (by introducing alternative economic possibilities, for instance), establishing some sort of compelling alternative to the clan system (an action that would weaken the pirates' organizational structure and feeling of solidarity), and eradicating the base camps. Diligent efforts must also be made to prevent the Somali pirates from acquiring outside sources of sponsorship and support. The danger is that al Qaeda (or some other terrorist group) will seek involvement in the enterprise, especially since Somalia is an Islamic country. Al Qaeda has experience both in international shipping and allegedly the piracy affecting Southeast Asia.

Above all, we must not ignore this contemporary African piracy or underestimate its potential severity simply because we arrogantly assume that pirates in small speedboats (the Somalis' raiding craft of choice) can do little harm. Indeed, one of the vital lessons the history of the golden age of piracy imparts is that pirates can do serious damage with what seem to be unformidable naval assets. As in the case study of the Barbary corsairs, it is ultimately the support system—based on the previously mentioned five fundamental factors—that determines the success of piracy.

# 5

# The International Community Cannot Ignore Piracy in Somalia

*Aidan Hartley*

*Aidan Hartley is a columnist for the* Spectator, *a weekly British magazine that has been published since 1828.*

*The civil war in Somalia that has resulted in hundreds of thousands of deaths has been ignored by the international community, leading to the rise of piracy. Somali piracy, which is costing shipping companies millions and forcing them to rethink routes near the Somali coast, is alleged to be funding terrorism and may have links to the government as well. Somali leaders claim they cannot stop piracy because of a lack of resources, despite Western aid in the form of tens of millions of dollars and shared intelligence. Al-Shabaab is the only group in Somalia that publicly declares it will end piracy, but the militant group is listed by the United States as a terrorist organisation linked to al Qaeda.*

The ceaseless piracy off Somalia's shores—another . . . tanker was hijacked—is giving rise to a modern, real-life version of the novel *Scoop*. Evelyn Waugh's book is set in Africa's troubled state of Ishmaelia, where one foreign correspondent breaks a big story from a place called Laku. As soon as it is published, Fleet Street editors begin clamouring for copy from Laku, so the press corps rush into the jungle where they become utterly lost. No wonder. It turns out laku means

Aidan Hartley, "What I Learned from the Somali Pirates," *Spectator*, December 6, 2008, pp. 18–19. Copyright © 2008 by *The Spectator*. Reproduced by permission of *The Spectator*.

'I don't know' in Ishmaelite—and the correspondent is writing secretly from his hotel room in the capital.

Somalia today is a bit like Laku. Editors are begging for stories about the pirates' latest catch; about the Saudi supertanker still being held hostage [the ship was freed in January 2009] at anchor off the eastern Somali coast; about the chemical tanker *Biscaglia*, which was nabbed in the Gulf of Aden. But if they were honest, instead of rushing out to Somalia to be kidnapped—like the four poor journalists abducted last week [November 2008]—the press corps would simply confess, 'I don't know.' There are too many laptop bombardiers writing acres of colour and analysis from the safety of London and Nairobi about this latter-day Laku. It's time to sit back and consider the real story.

---

*The pirate gangs, it turns out, are organised by ex-fishermen who got very annoyed by the way international boats poached Somalia's rich tuna-fishing grounds and dumped toxic waste along its ungoverned shores.*

---

The first obvious truth is that the pirates are making millions and shipping companies are beginning to avoid the Suez route in favour of the longer, more expensive one around the Cape of Good Hope, because nothing seems to deter the pirates. Patrolling by international navies has formed a kind of blockade, but look at the *Biscaglia*. At the first sniff of piracy, the British and Irish guards from the important-sounding Anti-Piracy Maritime Security Solutions company simply jumped overboard. All it took was five pirates approaching by daylight in a small speedboat.

## The Story Behind Somali Piracy

So what can be done? The first task is to understand the background. For years the world has ignored Somalia as a parochial African backwater involved in a nasty civil war. Hundreds of thousands have died of hunger and in hails of bullets. Our disregard for Somalia's suffering has resulted in a metastasised crisis that is spilling out of its borders. Piracy is just one symptom of several ways—you can add gun-running and terrorism to the list—in which Somalia's crisis will lash out at the world in 2009.

The allegation in many reports on Somalia is that piracy is funding militant Islamist forces fighting the local Western-backed government. The London-based Jane's Terrorism & Security Monitor claimed last month that the Islamists, known as al-Shabaab, had raised a force of 2,500 pirates to run guns and attack shipping.

---

*Somali piracy has become extremely efficient, with ransom payments organised via lawyers in regional African capitals.*

---

The real story is more bizarre. I know because I've met the pirates and spent 17 years covering Somalia. It's a frightening business—earlier this year [2008] my vehicle convoy was blown up by a roadside bomb and three people died—but fascinating. The pirate gangs, it turns out, are organised by ex-fishermen who got very annoyed by the way international boats poached Somalia's rich tuna-fishing grounds and dumped toxic waste along its ungoverned shores. In the early days they demanded poachers pay fines, but later they realised there was more money to be made from straightforward abductions.

Today the gangs recruit ordinary youths. Most rank-and-file pirates cannot even swim. Their only required skill is to shoot straight. These youths usually participate only in a couple of operations, hoping to make enough money to get asylum in the West. For example, if a young pirate makes around £20,000—his cut from two ransom pay-outs—he can persuade an ethnic Somali wife with a European Union passport to marry him and perhaps move to the United Kingdom. Staying in Somalia is not an option. Imams [Islamic leaders] at the mosques have declared piracy haram, forbidden under Islamic law. If the pirates want to buy goodies for themselves such as cell phones or cars, they find themselves being charged four times the going price.

Behind the pirates are godfathers and investors from clans closely related to Somalia's Western-backed president in Mogadishu, Abdullahi Yusuf. A veteran warlord with blood on his hands, Yusuf owes his life to a liver transplant from a British donor in a London hospital. Most of Yusuf's lieutenants are ethnic Somalis who hold British or European Union passports. Western countries including Britain have given substantial funding to Yusuf's forces, regarding him as an ally in the war on terror against the Islamist insurgents fighting his government.

## Pirate Links in the Government

Yusuf and his close circle hail from Puntland, Somalia's northeastern semiautonomous region. Estimates are that at least six ministers in the Puntland government, which is allied to Yusuf, are involved with the pirates—together with two former police chiefs and sundry mayors. Puntland's police forces were trained by the United Nations using British funding. But in some port towns pirate gangs are now paying police salaries. Puntland is the modern world's first genuine pirate state.

Somali piracy has become extremely efficient, with ransom payments organised via lawyers in regional African capitals. Ex-SAS officers [Special Air Service, a British Army special forces division] have been employed to deliver ransom payments in cash to the pirates on the high seas. My information is that the pirates behave like perfect gentlemen once the money is handed over and they always release the boats in good humour. For years, US Navy ships have skirmished with pirates and arrested them on the high seas. But in recent months I have heard repeated allegations that US Navy ships have enjoyed friendly relations with pirates off Puntland. In one story, pirates were invited aboard a US Navy ship for a cup of coffee and a smoke, while the Americans showed gang members national flags of ships that should be left alone.

---

*The only group in Somalia today that publicly declares it will end piracy is the militant al-Shabaab, because it says such crimes are forbidden under Islamic law.*

---

This all seems extremely odd unless American forces assume that the pirates are in some way linked to the Puntland authorities with whom they are allied. US intelligence works closely with the Puntland Intelligence Service, known as PIS, which has helped with anti-terrorism operations in the region. Last month [November 2008] al-Shabaab suicide bombers blew themselves up in two vehicles in Puntland's main port town of Bossaso. Their target was the PIS headquarters, and at the time of the attack there were almost certainly American agents in the building.

## Islamist Militants Fight Piracy

The West has given the authorities in Mogadishu and Puntland tens of millions of dollars and shared intelligence resources. Yet these Somali leaders claim they cannot stamp out piracy because they lack the resources. In 2006, when Mogadishu was ruled by Islamist militants, I witnessed forces of the Islamic courts jump into speedboats, zoom out to sea and arrest a gang of pirates who had seized a cargo ship. The Islamists paraded gang members on the portside before taking them off for harsh punishment. That was the end of piracy in that part of Somalia until Abdullahi Yusuf's government was installed during an invasion of Ethiopian troops, when attacks on shipping resumed.

The only group in Somalia today that publicly declares it will end piracy is the militant al-Shabaab, because it says such crimes are forbidden under Islamic law. Al-Shabaab is a Salafist group that was founded earlier this decade as a militia attached to an Islamic sharia court housed in a derelict Mogadishu shampoo factory known as Ifka Halane—which means 'Clean and Shiny'.

This Clean and Shiny militia has grown into the most frightening militant army in Africa today. It controls most of central and southern Somalia and all but a few blocks of Mogadishu itself.

The US lists al-Shabaab as a terrorist organisation linked to al-Qa'eda. Several air strikes have been launched to kill its leaders, but al-Shabaab still protects probably three senior al-Qa'eda operatives linked to terrorist bomb attacks across East Africa. During the past two years [2007 and 2008], while Western-backed forces battle[d] against insurgents, al-Shabaab has received growing financial support from overseas. Foreign jihadis have flocked to Somalia from Pakistan and now reports are that al-Qa'eda militants from Iraq have chosen Somalia as a new base from which to launch attacks. Unless more moderate groups can reach a peace deal urgently, al-Shabaab will overcome forces of the government and its allies—made up of Ethiopians and a small contingent of African peacekeepers in Mogadishu.

This may happen before Bush retires. It will be a ghastly legacy of his administration that has done so much to deepen Somalia's crisis. If al-Shabaab seizes Mogadishu, it will be the first time an ally of al-Qa'eda has captured a country since 9/11. The territory ahead is all Laku—but at least the scourge of piracy may be squashed.

# 6

# Local Fleets Should Handle Somali Pirates

*Peter Lehr*

*Peter Lehr is a lecturer in terrorism studies at the University of St. Andrews. He is the editor of* Violence at Sea: Piracy in the Age of Global Terrorism.

*Somali pirates have been getting bolder and bolder. However, a large Western naval presence in the region is unlikely to be effective. Instead, local navies must create regular patrols. In addition, the poaching of Somali fish must cease so that local fishermen have a chance to earn an honest living without turning to piracy.*

The seizure of the Saudi supertanker this week [November 2008] by the pirates of Somalia was their most audacious attack to date, but it was not their first. The pirates hit the headlines a little over three years ago, on November 5 2005, when they attempted to hijack the cruise liner *Seabourn Spirit* some 75 nautical miles off the coast of Somalia. This brazen but unsuccessful attack triggered the first wave of reports on piracy in the Gulf of Aden and off the coast of this beleaguered nation, which has not seen a central and effective government since the downfall of the Siad Barre regime in January 1991.

Soon, of course, the problem dropped off the media radar. It came back with a vengeance in April this year with the hijacking of the French luxury yacht *Le Ponant*. Its 30 crew members were kept hostage for eight days, and released apparently after a substantial amount of ransom had been paid. This time, media attention did not quickly die down: buoyed, no doubt, by the huge ransom paid in the *Le Ponant* case, Somali pirates embarked on an ambitious campaign, striking ever farther from their own shores. Late in September, Somali pirates succeeded in capturing the MV *Faina*, which was transporting 33 battle tanks, some 250 nautical miles off the coast of Somalia. The *Faina*'s crew of 21 [was] held hostage—except for its master, who died of a stroke soon after the hijacking. [Four months later the pirates released ship and crew after receiving ransom money.]

## Pirates See Themselves as Coast Guard

It has been quite a year for Somali pirates: 92 attacks have to date been attempted, with 36 successful hijackings and 268 crew members taken hostage. Given that the average ransom per vessel amounts to about $2m, it is hardly surprising that the port of Eyl, one of the major pirate lairs, has witnessed a veritable boom, with pirates feted by many as local heroes. Some observers estimate that Somali pirates reaped $30m in ransom during the first nine months of this year [2008].

> *The east African coastal waters of Somalia should ideally be patrolled by the naval forces of Kenya, Tanzania and other interested littoral states.*

Another sum is less frequently mentioned: the estimated $300m of fish poached in Somali waters annually by trawlers hailing from nations as far away as Taiwan—or France and Spain, for that matter. Seen from this perspective, it is hardly surprising that some pirate groups see themselves as defenders of Somali fishermen, giving their groups names such as National Volunteer Coast Guard of Somalia, or Somali Marines.

Their modus operandi is telling, too. The pirates have reached a technical and nautical sophistication matching that of many "real" coast guards all over the world: Somali pirates operate from mother ships, probably small freighters or local dhows [a type of sailing vessel] which enable them to strike so far out at sea. They use satellite phones and GPS as navigational aids, and once they spot their prey they attack it in wolfpack-style, swarming the targeted vessel with fast fibreglass boats and halting its passage by firing AK-47 salvoes or even rocket-propelled grenade rounds. Then they board the vessel, and the maritime hostage scenario begins.

## Locals, Regional Navies, Must Patrol Somali Waters

So steeply has the situation in the Gulf of Aden and along the 2,000-mile coast of Somalia deteriorated that the EU [European Union] has initiated a "close support protection system" for vessels transiting these perilous waters. The limitations of that system, and the scale of the challenge for anyone attempting to chase the pirates from the water, was made plain on Monday [November 17, 2008, following] the seizure of the *Sirius Star* outside the EU safe corridor. In any case, deploying western naval squadrons on a continuous basis might not be the best solution. Rather, regional navies or coast guards should be encouraged to pool their resources in order to conduct anti-piracy patrols, modelled on the Malacca Strait Patrol—which, conducted by the navies of Indonesia, Malaysia, Singapore and Thailand, resulted in a noticeable decrease of piracy in this former hot spot. This [accomplishment] was not lost on Egypt, which recently called upon the Red Sea states to inaugurate a similar combined effort in the Gulf of Aden. The east African coastal waters of Somalia should ideally be patrolled by the naval forces of Kenya, Tanzania and other interested littoral states [that is, states bordering the waterway]. The role of western navies could be to lend technical assistance and expertise, as well as provide some secondhand patrol vessels if required. This will be costly, but cheaper than keeping up a substantial western naval presence for the foreseeable future, overstretching military resources further still.

However, it should be pointed out that conducting antipiracy patrols in these waters can only ever be half of the solution. The other is to protect Somali waters against illegal fishing, thus giving local fishermen a fair chance to earn a living without turning to criminality. With all the focus on piracy and the "lure of easy money", it is all but forgotten that the majority of Somali fishermen do just that—try to earn a decent living against all odds, and now more and more often in the crossfire of pirates and navies. A deadly catch indeed.

# 7

# The Indian Navy Should Engage Pirates Who Threaten Indian Nationals

*Nitin Pai*

*Nitin Pai is an Indian journalist. Publications he has written for include* The Daily Mail, Mint, The Friday Times, *and* The Indian Express.

*Piracy in Somali waters has reached such dangerous levels that naval vessels from around the world are traveling to the region to stop it. Yet India's navy has not been dispatched to Somali waters, though India has important interests in the region. India must send its forces to aid in the containment of piracy. In addition, India should use its military to rescue Indian nationals held hostage by Somali pirates.*

According to the International Maritime Bureau, pirates have attacked 69 ships off the coast of Somalia since January of this year [2008]. They hijacked 27 and are currently holding 11 of them for ransom. Along with the ships and their cargo, they are holding more than 200 sailors hostage, of whom at least 18, including Captain P.K. Goyal of MT *Stolt Valor*, are Indian nationals. At least two Indian owned ships have been lost [in] these waters since 2006. A piracy-powered economy has developed in the Puntland region of Somalia, astride a corridor that carries a significant part of the world's—and India's—seaborne trade.

Clearly, piracy off Somalia presents a threat not only to international commerce and security, but also to humanitarian relief operations.

---

*Anyone who wishes to act against the pirates is legally allowed to do so.*

---

Humanitarian assistance to Somalia is under threat as the World Food Programme's shipments have been suspended after coming under attack. Indeed, the ransom-driven economy, entrenched warlordism, [and] radical Islamic militancy make the country a conducive breeding ground for international terrorism, turning the region into a watery Afghanistan.

At a time when the global economy is reeling under the weight of a widening financial crisis, additional risk and insurance premiums for the shipping trade are something the world, and certainly India, could do without.

## Someone Must Stop the Pirates

Both the UN Security Council and the president of Somalia have called for the international community to take an interest in patrolling the region. According to Seth Weinberger, a strategic affairs commentator, *suo motu* action [action taken on one's own initiative] against pirates has legal sanction under international law. "Piracy is one of the clearest examples of *jus cogens*, a preemptory norm that creates a crime for which there is no possible justification and for which there is universal jurisdiction. Thus, anyone who wishes to act against the pirates is legally allowed to do so.

"However, that creates a problem—in the absence of a specific jurisdiction, no one has the responsibility or strong incentive to act (why should one state bear the cost of enforcement when the cost of piracy falls on many?)"

As long as the pirate attacks were distributed in time and space, they remained under the threshold of international attention. But in the last few months [prior to October 2008], the pirates of Puntland have made the strategic mistake of becoming too successful.

They also ran out of luck. Among the vessels they hijacked was one carrying a huge arms shipment, and another, something altogether more mysterious (variously speculated to involve chemical weapons or radioactive material). And suddenly, the world's navies with the capability to get there—save India's—decided that it was time to go pirate hunting (or, at the very least, pirate watching) in the Red Sea. The US navy is already there. The Russian navy is on its way (and may well demonstrate some muscle in the days ahead). Last month, French special forces rescued two of their nationals in a daring commando operation. The European Union "is setting up an anti-piracy taskforce to help protect the lawless sea lanes off east Africa." So is NATO [North Atlantic Treaty Organization].

Among the tasks assigned to the Combined Task Force 150 (CTF-150)—an international naval task force [including] US, British, French, Pakistani and Bahraini ships—are maritime security operations in the Gulf of Aden, Gulf of Oman, the Arabian Sea, Red Sea and the Indian Ocean. While its purpose is to deny the use of the seas to smugglers and terrorists, the main problem in the area under its watch is piracy.

*The Indian government is demonstrating an inexplicable reluctance to dispatch the Indian Navy to the waters off Somalia.*

CTF-150 doesn't have enough ships to secure one of the world's busiest shipping lanes. So it advises large, slower vessels to travel in convoys so that it can better watch over them.

But since this is not always possible, around one in 500 ships falls victim to pirates. Since the monthly traffic is around 1,500, pirates succeed in raiding three or four ships each month.

# India Should Intervene Against Somali Pirates

Amid all this, the Indian government is demonstrating an inexplicable reluctance to dispatch the Indian Navy to the waters off Somalia. The UPA [United Progressive Alliance, India's ruling political coalition] government has been sitting on an Indian Navy proposal to secure Indian maritime interests off Somalia. According to Defence Minister A.K. Antony, "as a policy, the government would not carry out hot pursuit of pirates, as it had wider implications." It is hard to understand what "wider implications" Mr Antony is worried about when even the UN Security Council, through its resolution 1816, adopted with Somalia's consent in June 2008, authorised for a period of six months "all necessary means" to suppress acts of piracy.

Not only does the Indian government's pusillanimity [cowardice] disregard the threat to India's interests in the region, it also ignores the fact that a century ago, it was the (British) Indian navy that used to secure the Red Sea. In a report to the US Library of Congress, [Stanford University professor of political science] David Laitin states that "during the prime ministership of William Gladstone in the 1880s, it was decided that the Indian government should be responsible for administering the Somaliland protectorate because the Somali coast's strategic location on the Gulf of Aden was important to India. Customs taxes helped pay for India's patrol of Somalia's Red Sea Coast." More recently, the Indian Navy dispatched a three-ship task force to those waters in 1992, in support of a US-led international intervention in the wake of Somalia's civil war. According to the Indian Navy, it "spent a total of 347 ship days maintaining vigil along the Somali coast and ports during 1992–93." In addition, it supported the de-induction of Indian blue helmets [neutral members of UN peacekeeping forces] from Somalia in 1994.

Seen against India's readiness to contribute troops for UN peacekeeping operations around the world—in places where India has little at stake—the UPA government's refusal to authorise the Navy to protect India's interests is all the more incongruous.

---

*If commercial negotiations are unable to secure their release, then surely India can't abandon its nationals to the mercies of Somali pirates?*

---

Indeed, it underlines a lack of appreciation of the role of the armed forces and the use of military power at a fundamental level. As this particular case highlights, even the oft-cited fig leaf of the need for UN authorisation before India deploys its armed forces cannot cover up the sorry state of defence policymaking. A self-assured power would use military force when it is called for, regardless of international opinion, like India did in East Pakistan in 1971, Sri Lanka in 1987 and Maldives in 1988.

More recently, the Indian navy evacuated over 1,700 of its nationals from Lebanon in June 2006, in the wake of war between Israel and the Hezbollah militia. The Lebanon operation underlines what ought to be a tenet of India's foreign policy—that India is the ultimate protector of the lives of its citizens, wherever they might be on the planet.

## Indian Nationals Must Be Protected

The Indian sailors currently held hostage might have been sailing on Hong Kong-registered ships belonging to Japanese owners. But if commercial negotiations are unable to secure their release, then surely India can't abandon its nationals to the mercies of Somali pirates? Instead of ruling out this option or that, as Mr Antony has done, the policy of the Indian government must be to keep all options on the table.

It is in India's interests to work with the international maritime forces to contain the Somali pirates. There is a clear case to deploy the Indian Navy in the Red Sea off the coast of Somalia, with rules of engagement that include hot pursuit. Indeed, there is a clear case to task the marine commandos with hostage-rescue missions where Indian ships and nationals are taken hostage.

# 8

# Military Courts Need to Be Established to Deal with Piracy

*David B. Rivkin, Jr., and Lee A. Casey*

*David B. Rivkin, Jr. and Lee A. Casey are lawyers in Washington, D.C. They both served in the Justice Department under presidents Ronald Reagan and George H.W. Bush.*

*One difficulty in dealing with pirates is in figuring out who has jurisdiction to prosecute them. A solution is to use universal jurisdiction: the idea that any state may punish actions which violate certain norms of international law. Unfortunately, many European nations treat pirates as common criminals, which makes it impossible for military personnel to detain them. Turning them over to Somali authorities is also problematic, given the disarray of the Somali government. The West therefore needs to find a better way to balance the rights of pirates with the rights of their potential victims.*

On Saturday [November 15, 2008], off the coast of East Africa, pirates seized their largest catch ever: a giant Saudi-owned oil tanker called the *Sirius Star*. The brazen attack came on the heels of the capture of a Ukrainian vessel (loaded with armaments destined for Kenya) by Somali pirates in September. Humanitarian food shipments into Somalia have had naval escort for nearly a year—evidence of how

David B. Rivkin, Jr. and Lee A. Casey, "Pirates Exploit Confusion About International Law," *Wall Street Journal Online*, November 19, 2008. Copyright © 2008 Dow Jones & Company, Inc. All rights reserved. Reprinted with permission of The Wall Street Journal.

much the security of sea-lanes has eroded. Media reports suggest that Somali pirates have already attacked more than 80 ships in 2008.

## Piracy Is a Threat to Civilized Order

These are unprecedented and dangerous developments. Suppressing piracy and the slave trade, accomplished by the last quarter of the 19th century, were among mankind's great civilizing achievements. These were brought about by major maritime powers such as Great Britain and the United States. Indeed, in the American republic's earliest days, President Jefferson dispatched the infant U.S. Navy to confront the Barbary pirates, both on shore and at sea.

By the 1970s, as part of a growing chaos in [areas] of Africa and Asia, incidents of piracy began to pick up. But it was not until the 21st century that piracy ... experienced a meteoric rise, with the number of attacks increasing by double-digit rates per year. Last year, according to the International Maritime Bureau, 263 actual and attempted pirate attacks took place. Large maritime areas have now become known as pirate havens, where mariners can expect to be routinely molested. The Victorian self-confidence that drove pirates from the seas is gone.

---

*Capturing pirates is not the critical problem. Rather, the issue is how to handle those in captivity.*

---

Twenty-first century economics being what they are, the pirates have been more interested in the payment of ransom by anxious owners and insurers than in the vessels or their cargoes. Piracy is nonetheless a vicious and violent activity that exposes the world's merchant mariners to additional risk of death or injury. Even more fundamentally, the dramatic surge in piracy is, like terrorism, part of a broad challenge to civilization and international order.

Experience—especially that of colonial America—suggests that a few sporadic antipirate efforts will not be enough to solve the problem. Only a dedicated naval campaign, along with a determined effort to close the pirates' safe havens, will succeed in sending piracy back to the history books.

## Prosecuting Pirates Is Difficult

There has been some progress on this front. The North Atlantic Treaty Organization has dispatched a formidable multinational force—including British, Italian and Greek ships—to join the American, French, Canadian and Danish vessels already cruising off Somalia's vast coastline. France has also aggressively pursued pirates, freeing captured vessels and hostages.

Capturing pirates is not the critical problem. Rather, the issue is how to handle those in captivity. Traditionally, pirates fell within that category of illegitimate hostiles that once included slave traders, brigands on the roads and, in wartime, unprivileged or "unlawful" enemy combatants. As Judge Nicholas Trott, presiding over a pirate trial, explained in 1718: "It is lawful for any one that takes them, if they cannot with safety to themselves bring them under some government to be tried, to put them to death." This law, of course, has changed since the 18th century. Pirates, brigands and unlawful combatants must now be tried before they can be punished.

One solution would be for the capturing state to press charges based on the much misunderstood and abused principle of "universal" jurisdiction. This is the notion that any state may criminalize and punish conduct that violates certain accepted international-law norms. Although its application in most circumstances is dubious—there is very little actual state practice supporting the right of one state to punish the nationals of a second for offenses against the citizens of a third—piracy is one area where a strong case for universal jurisdiction can be made (if only because piratical activities often take place on the high seas, beyond any state's territorial jurisdiction).

Moreover, given the nature of naval operations, discerning who is a pirate is usually a much easier task than separating Taliban and al Qaeda members from innocent bystanders. This fact, all things being equal, should make the task of prosecuting captured pirates an easier process, both from a legal and public-relations perspective.

## Europe Has Abandoned the Legal Tools for Fighting Piracy

The key problem is that America's NATO allies have effectively abandoned the historical legal rules permitting irregular fighters to be tried in special military courts (or, in the case of pirates, admiralty courts) in favor of a straightforward criminal-justice model. Although piracy is certainly a criminal offense, treating it like bank robbery or an ordinary murder case presents certain problems for Western states.

To begin with, common criminals cannot be targeted with military force. There are other issues as well. Last April [2008] the British Foreign Office reportedly warned the Royal Navy not to detain pirates, since this might violate their "human rights" and could even lead to claims of asylum in Britain. Turning the captives over to Somali authorities is also problematic—since they might face the head- and hand-chopping rigors of Shariah [Islamic religious] law. Similar considerations have confounded U.S. government officials in their discussions of how to confront this new problem of an old terror at sea.

In the last few years, France determined to return its pirate prisoners to Somalia based on assurances of humanitarian treatment. The U.S. has, of course, rendered terror prisoners to foreign governments based on similar assurances, and only time will tell whether they are genuine. An equally important question is whether the transfer of captured pirates to local authorities will result in prosecution at all. In many areas, local governments may be subject to corruption or intimidation by strong pirate gangs.

One thing is certain: As in the war on terror, the new campaign against piracy will test the mettle of Western governments. It will also require them to balance the rights of lawbreakers against the indisputable rights of the law-abiding to not live their lives in danger and fear.

# 9

# The U.S. Should Reconfigure Its Navy or Coast Guard to Deal with Piracy

## Yoav Gortzak and Robert Farley

*Yoav Gortzak is an assistant professor of political science at Arizona State University. Robert Farley is an assistant professor at the Patterson School of Diplomacy and International Commerce, University of Kentucky.*

*To fight piracy effectively, the U.S. Navy would need to purchase smaller, more maneuverable ships. It would also need to refocus its mission, changing its focus from large conflicts to smaller-scale security and policing. These changes would be difficult and expensive, though not impossible. Antoher solution would be to expand the role of the Coast Guard to include anti-piracy activities in foreign waters. Since the Coast Guard's mission already involves policing and security, this second option might ultimately be more effective.*

A Navy dedicated to a serious anti-piracy mission would have to differ considerably from the current composition of the United States Navy [USN]. An anti-pirate USN would rely less on aircraft carriers, expensive surface warfare vessels, and submarines than the current force. Small, relatively inexpensive ships like the Littoral Combat Ship (LCS), or even smaller and less expensive corvette-sized ships, would take precedence over the larger and more powerful vessels. An ex-

Yoav Gortzak and Robert Farley, "The Responsibilities of Hegemony: U.S. Naval Doctrine and Piracy in Southeast Asia," *Paper Presented at the Annual Meeting of the International Studies Association*, March 22, 2006. Reproduced by permission of the authors.

pansion in the number of ships and a preference for ships useful in anti-piracy work would expand the geographic reach of the United States Navy and enable it to patrol wider areas with greater care. This program would entail, for instance, a rejection or reduction of the submarine acquisitions outlined in the 2005 Quadrennial Defense Review, as well as the replacement of planned DD(X) [a destroyer ship] acquisitions with larger numbers of the proposed LCS, which has gone into production.

---

*The US Navy has difficulty operating against pirates because its organizational culture does not favor constabulary missions like anti-piracy.*

---

## To Fight Piracy, the Navy Needs Smaller Ships

The LCS specializes in combat in shallow coastal areas threatened by mines, submarines, and swarming small boats. The LCS increases USN combat capability in littoral [coastal] areas, clearing the way for other ships to deliver ordnance [supplies] or personnel in a hostile environment. The LCS would increase the capacity of the United States to intervene against targets without the need to use local allies as staging bases. It can be equipped with a set of "modules" that allow it to perform a large variety of different missions. Because of this flexibility, the LCS represents a genuine increase in the capacity of the United States to fight piracy and piracy-related terrorism.

The USN can purchase the relatively inexpensive LCS in large numbers. Compared to the cost of other surface combatants, especially the DD(X), the LCS is inexpensive, meaning that the USN could acquire a relatively large number of these vessels. Each ship is large enough to contain the personnel, weapons, and sensor arrays necessary for patrolling endangered areas. The USN has considered purchasing up to eighty-two LCSs at a cost of $260 million each. Interestingly enough, however, the USN does not plan to use all or even most of its LCS acquisitions in an anti-piracy role. Rather, the USN hopes that the vessels will prove useful in conflict against China or other high-intensity applications. The United States Navy could also slow or halt the retirement of the Oliver Hazard Perry class frigates. Although no longer suitable for front line service in high intensity conflicts, the frigates would be ideal for a maritime maintenance mission. The Navy no longer uses the frigates to defend carrier battle groups, meaning that at least thirty frigates could be employed for anti-piracy and anti-terrorism work. An additional ten frigates maintained by the Naval Reserve Force could also be used to fight piracy and terrorism.

## To Fight Piracy, the Navy Must Rethink Its Mission

The transformation of the United States Navy into an organization capable of undertaking a significant anti-piracy mission would also have to include a major shift in the mindset of the USN, from concern about high intensity combat at sea and in the littorals to low intensity and constabulary roles. At the present time, material scarcity is only part of the reason ... the US Navy is not well prepared for taking on a broader anti-piracy mission. The US Navy has difficulty operating against pirates because its organizational culture docs not favor constabulary missions like anti-piracy. The current "organizational frame" of the United States Navy does not identify piracy as a significant problem.

A significant shift in the "organizational frame" of the United States Navy, therefore, would have to take place for an anti-piracy mission to become feasible. Although such a transformation, even for a major military organization, is not unheard of—in the aftermath of the Napoleonic Wars the British Royal Navy shifted from a force built around ships-of-the-line to a force of frigates and cruisers, smaller ships capable of patrolling sea lanes at a relatively low cost—significant institutional resistance should be expected against such a transformation, as there are strong vested interests in maintaining the current organizational frame of the United States Navy. Interestingly, this organizational frame sets the USN apart not only from hegemonic navies in the past such as the Royal Navy, which identified piracy as a major problem, but also from its own founding mission, which was rooted in an anti-piracy mission.

---

*The Coast Guard already has the intellectual tools and organizational outlook required for anti-piracy.*

---

The United States Navy has shifted its focus over the last fifteen years from peer competitor confrontation [conflicts with large, powerful navies, like Russia's] to littoral combat and Joint Warfare [better integration with other branches of the military]. This change has had a significant effect on the operations of the Navy, even if the concentration on high intensity operations remains the same. Nevertheless, the Navy has changed, and it is not unreasonable to think that the Navy might continue to change based on the interests and needs of the United States. In order to become an effective anti-piracy and anti-terrorism organization, the Navy must identify maritime maintenance and constabulary operations as problems. Although the material structure of the USN is not ideal for such operations, it has the capabilities to carry them out. . . .

## The Coast Guard Could Fight Piracy

Reorienting the United States Navy toward an anti-piracy mission would prove enormously expensive, and would likely detract from the capacity of the USN to perform its other missions, including Joint action in littoral areas. Rather than reinvent the Navy, the United States could take advantage of a military organization that already engages in many of the activities associated with the prevention of piracy. The mission of the United States Coast Guard already includes such tasks as coastal defense, offshore law enforcement, drug interdiction, and search and rescue, all of which are applicable to fighting piracy. Moreover, the Coast Guard employs a large number of relatively small, inexpensive ships. As noted previously, inexpensive, low capability ships are ideal for deterring piracy. Since most pirates lack the firepower to challenge a military vessel of any size, even a small ship can effectively prevent attacks.

The expansion of the mission of the Coast Guard would require an expansion in the size of the Coast Guard. However, this project would have several advantages over an effort to transform the Navy. The Coast Guard already pursues the mission of maritime security maintenance. While forcing the Navy to adopt an anti-pirate mission would require a transformation of organizational framing, the Coast Guard already has the intellectual tools and organizational outlook required for anti-piracy. Expanding the Coast Guard would also allow the Navy to pursue its warfighting capabilities, both in the littorals and in the open sea. Naval training and organizational focus could remain on its traditional mission, while the Coast Guard pursued maritime security missions.

As mentioned above, one way to expand the Coast Guard would be to transfer the existing Oliver Hazard Perry frigates to Coast Guard control. These vessels would immediately become the largest, most powerful, and longest ranged ships in the Coast Guard arsenal, and would allow the Coast Guard to pursue the maritime security mission in short order. Thirty "FIG-7" ships remain in commission with the US Navy, with an additional ten serving in the Naval Reserve Force. As the LCS will fulfill some of the roles traditionally accorded to frigates and the Arleigh Burke destroyers will assume others, the Navy can spare these ships. Forty ships, according to the calculations described earlier in the paper, would go far to allowing the Coast Guard to patrol the major choke points of international maritime commerce. Of course, Coast Guard funding would need to increase in order to crew and maintain these ships.

Expanding the Coast Guard would not solve all of the problems associated with an anti-piracy mission. The legal constraints associated with sovereignty and territorial waters would still restrict the deployment of US vessels. However, as the Coast Guard is not a warfighting organization, the United States might find it easier to convince Southeast Asian and other countries to relax legal restrictions.

# 10

# To Fight Piracy at Sea, First Fight Lawlessness on Land

*Rama Anom Kurniawan*

*Rama Anom Kurniawan works at the Directorate of Treaties for Political, Security and Territorial Affairs at the Foreign Ministry of Indonesia.*

*United Nations resolutions allowing other nations to enter Somali waters to fight piracy will not solve the problem by themselves. Instead, Indonesia's experience suggests that piracy is planned on land and that lawlessness on land contributes to piracy. The international community, therefore, needs to confront Somalia's political instability as well as take action against pirates at sea.*

It has been more than 15 years since the security and stability issues in Somalia were first brought to the attention of the UN Security Council through its Resolution 733 of 1992. Recent developments have also shown that this problem, which has become an international concern, is far from settled since stability in the region, Somalia specifically, remains elusive.

The waters off the coast of Somalia today are one of the world's more dangerous zones. The violent acts of piracy and armed robbery against vessels off those shores and the serious threat those acts pose to the prompt, safe and effective delivery of humanitarian aid to Somalia, to international naviga-

Rama Anom Kurniawan, "Piracy An Extension of Somalia's Lawless Land," *Jakarta Post Online*, December 17, 2008. Reproduced by permission.

tion, to safe passage along commercial maritime routes and to fishing conducted there have become of grave concern to the international community.

In order to address these issues, the UNSC [UN Security Council] has responded promptly by endorsing a critical declaration, Resolution 1816 (2008) [allowing other states to enter Somali waters to fight pirates].

After the adoption of Resolution 1816 (2008), France, other European countries and other international partners have taken steps to implement that resolution by establishing a military presence off the coast of Somalia. But these steps have not provided positive results: Piracy and robbery in those waters continue unabated, and have even intensified recently.

The most recent act that surprised the world was the nervy hijacking of the loaded Saudi-owned crude oil tanker *Sirius Star*, whose ship and load was valued at nearly US$100 million, by pirates believed to originate from Somalia.

To reemphasize the actions needed to fully eradicate piracy and armed robbery off Somalia's coast, the UN Security Council passed another resolution, 1838, on Oct. 7, 2008, intended to strengthen the previous Resolution 1816.

---

*Law enforcement on land and the peaceful settlement of the problems on land [are] necessary to minimize incidents at sea.*

---

## Piracy Begins on Land

In light of the recent high-profile incidents, the international military presence in waters off the coast of Somalia is intended to suppress the chronic piracy.

Though well intentioned, people have misunderstood that the issue of armed robbery against ships at sea is a purely maritime issue.

This misunderstanding needs to be addressed. In Indonesia's experience, most armed robberies against ships are planned on land and goods stolen are generally sold or traded on land. Moreover, the pirates maintain a land base for their operations. Security problems in national territories, such as rebel forces, freedom fighters or paramilitaries, can provoke chronic piracy and other criminal acts at sea.

Indonesia has successfully taken action against armed robbery at sea in the Strait of Malacca, in its territorial waters off the Aceh coast. As a matter of fact, prior to 2004, much of the illegal activity which occurred in the Strait of Malacca was associated with the Free Aceh Movement (GAM) [unarmed separatist movement] and supported their cause.

The successful political settlement between Indonesia and GAM has contributed to reducing the number of illegal seizures and threats against ships in those waters.

This may be the case in Somalia where existing threats in coastal waters are not random actions at sea but generated on land. Therefore law enforcement on land and the peaceful settlement of the problems on land [are] necessary to minimize incidents at sea.

---

*The international community should support the appeal for greater international contributions and cooperation in protecting the humanitarian convoys bound for Somalia. . . .*

---

## Somalia Needs Principled Help

Notwithstanding, I believe that no country can mount a defense on its own to tackle the newly emerging nontraditional security threats. Cooperation with other states is required: in the case of Somalia, which lacks the military power to defend herself, Resolution 1816 is necessary. Nevertheless, a set of principles should be kept in mind in dealing with such a cooperative effort in maritime security.

First, such cooperation should be based on respect for the sovereignty of the coastal state.

Second, any measures undertaken in the territorial waters of a coastal state regarding maritime security should be managed through a bilateral mechanism between the coastal state and other involved states.

Third, a comprehensive operation to eliminate armed robbery and other criminal acts against ships at sea should take into account the relevant operations on land, both in planning and in trading.

As a conclusion, we should not see piracy off the coast of Somalia as a stand-alone problem. Rather, it is an extension of the continuing political instability and lawlessness in Somalia itself.

Therefore, the international community should support the appeal for greater international contributions and cooperation in protecting the humanitarian convoys bound for Somalia and in repressing piracy and armed robbery at sea in conformity with international law, in particular the 1982 UN Convention on the Law of the Sea, and Security Council Resolution 1816. These instruments are both necessary and adequate to address this threat.

# 11

# Somali "Pirates" Are Actually Trying to Stop Illegal Dumping and Fishing

*Johann Hari*

*Johann Hari is a playwright and journalist. He writes a regular column for* The Independent *and* The Huffington Post. *In 2007, Amnesty International named him Newspaper Journalist of the Year for his reporting on the war in Congo.*

*Golden Age pirates were rebelling against the cruelty and tyranny of the Royal Navy. Similarly, Somali pirates are fighting against injustice. When the Somali government collapsed, European vessels began illegally fishing and even dumping toxic waste in Somali waters. When Somali fishermen tried to stop these activities, they were labeled as pirates. Thus, while some of the Somali "pirates" are thugs, many are merely trying to defend their homes.*

Who imagined that in 2009, the world's governments would be declaring a new War on Pirates? As you read this, the British Royal Navy—backed by the ships of more than two dozen nations, from the US to China—is sailing into Somalian waters to take on men we still picture as parrot-on-the-shoulder pantomime villains. They will soon be fighting Somalian ships and even chasing the pirates onto land, into one of the most broken countries on earth. But behind the arrr-me-hearties oddness of this tale, there is an untold scandal. The people our governments are labelling as "one of the great menaces of our times" have an extraordinary story to tell—and some justice on their side.

## Golden Age Pirates Rebelled Against Injustice

Pirates have never been quite who we think they are. In the "golden age of piracy"—from 1650 to 1730—the idea the pirate as the senseless, savage Bluebeard that lingers today was created by the British government in a great propaganda heave. Many ordinary people believed it was false: pirates were often saved from the gallows by supportive crowds. Why? What did they see that we can't? In his book *Villains Of All Nations*, the historian Marcus Rediker pores through the evidence.

If you became a merchant or navy sailor then—plucked from the docks of London's East End, young and hungry— you ended up in a floating wooden Hell. You worked all hours on a cramped, half-starved ship, and if you slacked off, the all-powerful captain would whip you with the Cat O' Nine Tails. If you slacked often, you could be thrown overboard. And at the end of months or years of this, you were often cheated of your wages.

---

*As soon as the government was gone, mysterious European ships started appearing off the coast of Somalia, dumping vast barrels into the ocean.*

---

Pirates were the first people to rebel against this world. They mutinied—and created a different way of working on the seas. Once they had a ship, the pirates elected their captains and made all their decisions collectively, without torture. They shared their bounty out in what Rediker calls "one of the most egalitarian plans for the disposition of resources to be found anywhere in the eighteenth century."

They even took in escaped African slaves and lived with them as equals. The pirates showed "quite clearly—and subversively—that ships did not have to be run in the brutal and oppressive ways of the merchant service and the Royal Navy." This is why they were romantic heroes, despite being unproductive thieves.

## Europeans Dump Waste and Fish Illegally in Somali Waters

The words of one pirate from that lost age, a young British man called William Scott, should echo into this new age of piracy. Just before he was hanged in Charleston, South Carolina, he said: "What I did was to keep me from perishing. I was forced to go a-pirateing to live." In 1991, the government of Somalia collapsed. Its nine million people have been teetering on starvation ever since—and the ugliest forces in the Western world have seen this as a great opportunity to steal the country's food supply and dump our nuclear waste in their seas.

Yes: nuclear waste. As soon as the government was gone, mysterious European ships started appearing off the coast of Somalia, dumping vast barrels into the ocean. The coastal population began to sicken. At first they suffered strange rashes, nausea and malformed babies. Then, after the [2004] tsunami, hundreds of the dumped and leaking barrels washed up on shore. People began to suffer from radiation sickness, and more than 300 died.

Ahmedou Ould-Abdallah, the UN envoy to Somalia, tells me: "Somebody is dumping nuclear material here. There is also lead, and heavy metals such as cadmium and mercury—you name it." Much of it can be traced back to European hospitals and factories, who seem to be passing it on to the Italian mafia to "dispose" of cheaply. When I asked Mr Ould-Abdallah what European governments were doing about it, he said with a sigh: "Nothing. There has been no clean-up, no compensation, and no prevention."

At the same time, other European ships have been looting Somalia's seas of their greatest resource: seafood. We have destroyed our own fish stocks by overexploitation—and now we have moved on to theirs. More than $300m-worth of tuna, shrimp, and lobster are being stolen every year by illegal trawlers. The local fishermen are now starving. Mohammed Hussein, a fisherman in the town of Marka, 100km south of Mogadishu, told Reuters: "If nothing is done, there soon won't be much fish left in our coastal waters."

---

*Did we expect starving Somalians to stand passively on their beaches, paddling in our toxic waste, and watch us snatch their fish to eat in restaurants in London and Paris and Rome?*

---

## Somali "Pirates" Are Defending Their Waters

This is the context in which the "pirates" have emerged. Somalian fishermen took speedboats to try to dissuade the dumpers and trawlers, or at least levy a "tax" on them. They call themselves the Volunteer Coastguard of Somalia—and ordinary Somalis agree. The independent Somalian news site WardheerNews found 70 per cent "strongly supported the piracy as a form of national defence."

No, this doesn't make hostage-taking justifiable, and yes, some are clearly just gangsters—especially those who have held up World Food Programme supplies. But in a telephone interview, one of the pirate leaders, Sugule Ali: "We don't consider ourselves sea bandits. We consider sea bandits [to be] those who illegally fish and dump in our seas." William Scott would understand.

Did we expect starving Somalians to stand passively on their beaches, paddling in our toxic waste, and watch us snatch their fish to eat in restaurants in London and Paris and Rome? We won't act on those crimes—the only sane solution to this problem—but when some of the fishermen responded by disrupting the transit-corridor for 20 per cent of the world's oil supply, we swiftly send in the gunboats.

The story of the 2009 war on piracy was best summarised by another pirate, who lived and died in the fourth century BC. He was captured and brought to Alexander the Great, who demanded to know "what he meant by keeping possession of the sea." The pirate smiled, and responded: "What you mean by seizing the whole earth; but because I do it with a petty ship, I am called a robber, while you, who do it with a great fleet, are called emperor." Once again, our great imperial fleets sail—but who is the robber?

# 12

# Terrorists and Pirates Are Similar But Not the Same

*Benerson Little*

*Benerson Little is a former Navy SEAL. He is now a consultant and writer specializing in maritime and naval issues. He is the author of* The Sea Rover's Practice: Pirate Tactics and Techniques, 1630–1730 *and of* The Buccaneer's Realm: Pirate Life on the Spanish Main, 1674–1688.

*The purpose of terrorism is to create a political effect. Pirates may occasionally use political rhetoric, but they seldom act on it—their main goal is personal gain. Dealing with pirates and terrorists, however, does require similar tactics. In both cases, direct military action is needed in concert with an assault on underlying causes, such as poverty and government instability.*

Regarding the argument that the pirate is a terrorist, or that piracy is equivalent to terrorism, we should very briefly examine the ultimate purpose of both terrorism and piracy. In the case of terrorism, the purpose is political, and its means, including the use of violence to create a state of terror, are focused on that end. Many analysts tend to forget that terrorists do not kill people and blow up buildings primarily to get attention. They do it to get a reaction, preferably one that will turn a local or even an international population against a government, people, corporation, other organization, or idea, which in turn helps fill terrorist ranks and helps

Benerson Little, "Guest Post: Pirates Are Not Terrorists, But the Prevention of Both Are Similar," *MountainRunner.us*, December 15, 2008. Reproduced by permission of the author.

achieve political ends. For example, Al-Qaeda must have seen the US invasion of Iraq as a gift from heaven. Attention via violence is just the vehicle.

---

*The pirate who did occasionally spout political or rebellious rhetoric seldom bothered to raise a hand in actual rebellion or in other political purpose. . . .*

---

## Piracy Is Not Political

Piracy, on the other hand, is simply armed theft on the sea (and in the past, from the sea as well). It lacks a political purpose, although it can of course be used as a tactic or strategy to finance or otherwise support terrorism, unrelated criminal activity, insurgency, or even (in the past) state- or empire-building. Ideally, . . . the pirate would prefer that no exceptional knowledge of his activity come to light. His goal is not to become a martyr or spend his life in jail, but to enjoy his spoils. In most cases, when the pirate does use "terror," he is not engaging in terrorism, but is simply using fear [to] make his job easier, as does any armed thief. The incitement of fear, even to the extent of terror, helps prevent his prey from fighting back, and thus makes piracy more profitable, not to mention helps keep the pirate alive so that he can spend his gains. Beyond this, the pirate has no use for fear or terror. Were he to routinely engage in violence on the level of the terrorist—in terrorism, in other words—every hand would soon turn against him. Lacking a political purpose and a political base, he would soon find himself violently ostracized, except by those who rely immediately upon him for economic sustenance. There is a good reason, for example, that Somali pirates have so far treated their prisoners well. Further, the pirate generally does not seek to destroy states or economies, although on occasion in the past he has had a hand in this.

He requires functioning states and well-ordered economies, for they are the source of his prey—of his "profit by plunder," in other words.

---

*Both [piracy and terrorism] are best handled in their infancy ... but both are often overlooked or ignored until they are well-established.*

---

To be fair, there are some Marxist-based historians and economists who consider piracy as the result of class warfare, and thus a form of rebellion, and thus ultimately political. However, looking at piracy from antiquity to the present, although its purpose is invariably and by definition economic—plunder or ransom—it goes no further than this, no matter its inspiration, whether of poverty, other hardship, opportunism, or a combination thereof. Indeed, some scholars refer to the pirate as a mere parasite, although this is often too simple a description. The pirate who did occasionally spout political or rebellious rhetoric seldom bothered to raise a hand in actual rebellion or in other political purpose, much less engage in what we today would refer to as "terrorism," notwithstanding his occasionally brutal treatment of his prey, including prisoners. (Much of the pirate's brutality was brought out in the search for plunder. Other was obviously the work of disturbed minds, but some likely originated in the need to seek revenge upon a scapegoat, lending support in some instances to the theory of class warfare. Still, such "terrorism" had no further political purpose.) On the few occasions when the pirate did engage in rebellion or participate in insurgency, it was often as a mercenary, and in any case, rebellion was not his original intent, nor did it extend to what we would refer to as terrorism. Even when he threatened or bribed a local government, it was not for political purpose, but to facilitate his ability to engage in piracy.

The pirate did not and does not actively seek to overthrow governments or change the world order, neither as rebel nor as terrorist. Economic gain via armed theft for private purpose was and is his goal. The occasional political rhetoric of a minority of his ilk was typically mere rationalization or "verbalized motive," as opposed to an indication of actual purpose of rebellion or political change, and it remains so today. Somali pirate spokesmen, for example, have spouted various rhetoric about taking revenge for the illegal fishing of their waters, but the goal of Somali pirates is primarily material gain for private purpose, not the righting of a wrong.

## Pirates and Terrorists Are Similar in Some Ways

All this being said, there are two critical similarities between piracy and terrorism. The first is in the two-pronged manner in which both are best dealt with. On the one hand, a combination of direct military (predominantly naval when dealing with piracy) and law enforcement action, including effective intelligence gathering and analysis, is required to deal with the immediate threat. In the case of piracy, this includes the protection of merchant shipping, the capture or destruction of pirates and their materiel (including mother ships), and the isolation or destruction of their bases (in the case of the Somalis, difficult, perhaps impossible without harming local populations). In parallel with these efforts, the underlying causes must be dealt with via a variety of coordinated means, including conventional diplomacy, public diplomacy, education, economic aid, amnesty programs, strengthening of local government, and other related means. In the case of Somalia, the failed state must be made to function again—an obviously difficult proposition lacking in substantive international support.

The second critical similarity between piracy and terrorism is their potential tenacity. Under the right circumstances, both can be difficult to eradicate if permitted to gain a foothold. Both are best handled in their infancy, so to speak, but both are often overlooked or ignored until they are well-established.

# 13

# States Can Do Little Against Maritime Terrorism and Piracy

*William Langewiesche*

*William Langewiesche is an American author and journalist. He is currently the international correspondent for the magazine* Vanity Fair, *but made his name as a national correspondent for* The Atlantic Monthly *magazine.*

*The ocean is chaotic and dangerous. A maritime terrorist attack on the United States by al Qaeda is a real threat. Such an attack might take the form of the bombing of a commercial or merchant ship. More dangerous, however, is the possibility that a merchant or container ship could be used to transport weapons of mass destruction to the mainland. Because of the lawlessness of the sea, monitoring ship traffic for such a threat is extremely difficult. The persistence of new forms of sophisticated piracy shows how hard it is for navies to impose order on the sea.*

For those of us who live ashore and are accustomed to the promise of orderly lives, it can be difficult to accept just how unruly the ocean has become. In earlier times, people were clearer about its savagery. For most of human history, with few exceptions, the open ocean was simply a forbidden zone, a place of horrors real and imagined, that was only occasionally crossed on accidental trips downwind, dangerously, and with no way home. The ocean was the great barrier isolating the continental populations and, incidentally, also protecting them from one another. . . .

## Terrorism by Sea Is a Serious Threat

In the 1990s, as the maritime disorder grew, officials had to struggle against smuggling and the occasional big oil spill, but they continued to see the ocean in tidy governmental terms as a place subject to civilization, where navies projected national power and merchant ships sailed, however reluctantly, under increasing technical restraints. It was a view of the world still possible at the end of the twentieth century—an illusion of progress and community that was demolished twenty-one months later, with the attack of September 11, 2001. Since then, in the United States, many officials have come to regard the ocean with grave concern, believing that a full-blown maritime attack would make those of September 11 seem puny by comparison, that such an attack currently poses the most serious threat to national security, and that when the attack comes, it will involve the use of merchant ships. They may well be right. Ships can deliver a big punch, and their importance to world commerce practically ensures that in the reactions that follow, major self-inflicted damage will be done. In any case, for officials now eyeing the sea, suddenly freedom no longer looks like control, and even a twelve-mile limit seems far too near.

---

*Osama bin Laden is said to own or control up to twenty aging freighters—a fleet dubbed the "al Qaeda Navy" by the tabloids.*

---

Out beyond the horizon, there is evidence that al Qaeda and related groups are indeed nautically minded, and have been since well before September 11. On January 3, 2000, al Qaeda and some of its affiliates conspired to ram a fiberglass workboat heavily loaded with explosives against a U.S. destroyer named *The Sullivans* in the Yemeni port of Aden. The attack was aborted after the boat nearly sank under the weight of the explosives. The terrorists learned their lesson. Later that same year, in the same port, they loaded a boat properly and blew a forty-foot hole through the hull of another destroyer, the *USS Cole*. Seventeen sailors were killed, and thirty-nine were wounded. It was early October 2000—September 11 minus eleven months. In response, the U.S. Navy tightened its warships' defenses. Other than that, the attack on the *Cole* had little effect. Again the terrorists appear to have learned a lesson—possibly about the inefficiency of hitting purely military targets, glorious though such targets may be.

Two years later another small boat darted out from the Yemeni shores, and it exploded against the *Limburg*, a French supertanker loaded with crude oil. The ship caught on fire and spilled oil, and one sailor was killed. This time the damage was magnified by increases in insurance costs for ships calling at Yemeni ports, along with a corresponding drop-off in traffic, as a result of which the Yemeni economy has suffered. True, if the goal was to hit at the West, this hardly constituted a major blow, but the sophistication of the choice to attack a civilian ship was noted with concern around the world, and it spread damage merely by raising the question of what would come next. A cruise ship full of Americans? A European ferry? A tanker in the Strait of Hormuz? A freighter off Gibraltar? Already the navies of the United States and its allies have their hands full with escort duties and patrols. And the ocean is a very big place. With deliberate preparation and the occasional well-placed attack, a few men with small boats can keep the navies churning for years.

## Merchant Ships May Be Used by Terrorists

But the real concern is not so much the vulnerability of merchant ships as it is their use by terrorist groups. Osama bin

Laden is said to own or control up to twenty aging freighters—a fleet dubbed the "al Qaeda Navy" by the tabloids. To skeptics who wonder why bin Laden would want to own so many freighters, the explanation quite simply is that he and his associates are in the shipping business. Given his need for anonymity, this makes perfect sense—and it reflects as much on the shipping industry as on al Qaeda that the details remain murky. Such systematic lack of transparency is what worries U.S. officials when they contemplate the sea. The al Qaeda ships are believed to have carried cement and sesame seeds, among other legitimate cargoes. In 1998 one of them delivered the explosives to Africa that were used to bomb the U.S. embassies in Kenya and Tanzania. But immediately before and afterward it was an ordinary merchant ship, going about ordinary business. As a result, that ship has never been found. Nor have any of the others.

One measure of American frustration is the executive order signed by President [George W.] Bush in July 2002 that expanded the U.S. Navy's authority to intercept merchant ships on the high seas. The target has always been larger than simply the al Qaeda fleet of freighters: the government maintains a watch list of several hundred suspect ships whose names are constantly being changed and painted over to avoid detection, and it recognizes that terrorists, with or without a crew's knowledge, may use almost any kind of ship, from a dhow to a supersized freighter. Therefore the search has been large—and enormously expensive. It has extended through much of the world's oceans and has been carried out by the navies of the United States and its allies. By rough calculation, NATO [North Atlantic Treaty Organization] forces so far have intercepted more than sixteen thousand ships, and they have boarded and searched about two hundred of them. For all that, there have been only a few rather modest successes.

For example, after an operation in July 2002 that involved warships and airplanes from four NATO nations (not including the United States), four suspected al Qaeda operatives were found on a couple of freighters in the Gulf of Oman and were transferred to a holding pen at the American base in Bagram, Afghanistan. The following month, fifteen Pakistani suspects on another ship were captured by the Italians in the Mediterranean after the ship's captain grew suspicious and turned them in. The ship had been renamed five times in the previous three years, most recently as the *Sara*. It was flagged in Tonga and owned by a Greek who operated it through a company named Nova Spirit, of Romania and Delaware. American officials said that the company was involved in human smuggling, an allegation that the owner vigorously denied. According to the captain, the Pakistanis had joined the ship in Casablanca, at the owner's insistence. Though they had claimed to be seamen and had carried seamen's documents, they demonstrated no knowledge of ships, and to a man grew seasick when the *Sara* sailed through a storm. The captain said that they threatened the crew. If so, as terrorists go, they were inept. Because they were found with false passports, large amounts of cash, maps of Italian cities, and unspecified evidence linking them to purported al Qaeda operatives in Europe, they were charged with conspiracy to engage in terrorist acts. Pakistan refuted the charges and claimed that Italian authorities had bungled the investigation. By the following summer, the Pakistanis' plight had drawn the attention of human rights activists, and in June 2003 they were freed.

---

*The fear on everyone's mind is that a nuclear device or some other weapon of mass destruction will pass through a port with little chance of being discovered.*

---

## Container Ships Are a Potential Threat

Italy took an even softer line in two other encounters. In February 2002, eight suspected al Qaeda terrorists disembarked from a Nova Spirit ship in Trieste with false documents and ultimately disappeared. A more bizarre ease had occurred several months earlier, in October 2001, when port police in the southern city of Gioia Tauro found a forty-three-year-old Egyptian-born Canadian citizen named Amid Farid Rizk inside a Maersk Sealand container. Rizk became known as "Container Bob." His box had been loaded in Port Said, Egypt, and was being transferred in Italy to a ship bound for Rotterdam, where it was scheduled to be transferred again, this time for the final destination of Halifax, Nova Scotia. It is said that Rizk was discovered when the Italian police heard him drilling additional ventilation holes. He was a man who apparently liked his comforts. When he emerged, he was clean-shaven, neatly dressed, and obviously well rested. The container was equipped with a bed, a toilet, a heater, a water supply, a cell phone, a satellite phone, and a laptop computer. Investigators also found cameras; a valid Canadian passport; maps and security passes for airports in Canada, Thailand, and Egypt; a Canadian aircraft-mechanic certificate; and an airline ticket from Montreal to Cairo via Rome.

---

*The new pirates . . . have emerged on a post-modern ocean, where identities have been mixed and blurred and the rules of nationality have been subverted.*

---

The use of containers to gain entry to North America is a well-established trick, part of the vast volume of human smuggling that relies on the far vaster volume of ordinary trade to penetrate the borders. And though the customers willing to transport themselves this way often arrive in very poor shape (sometimes dead), Cadillac containers like Rizk's have been seen before. Still, Rizk never adequately explained his setup or why, as a Canadian citizen, he had not simply flown. Upon his arrest he hired an attorney named Michele Filippo Italiano, whose services I can recommend. Italiano said that Rizk's decision to travel in a container was completely innocent: "He had fallen out with his brother-in-law in Cairo and feared he would be prevented from leaving Egypt." An Italian court released Rizk on bail in November 2001, at which point he vanished, leaving no trace.

In their frustration, U.S. authorities reacted angrily and remonstrated with the Italian government. But in a world of trouble, a more serious threat is posed by the inanimate cargo that containers may hold. The fear on everyone's mind is that a nuclear device or some other weapon of mass destruction will pass through a port with little chance of being discovered, and will subsequently be carried by truck or train with dead-on precision to any target desired. Despite their expanded ability to run intercepts, there is very little that the allied navies can do about it. Aboard the transporting ships, the containers are stacked tightly and high, and most are impossible to get at. Moreover, speed is the essence of the container business: the ships move fast and on schedule, and any act of interference that did not immediately produce results would raise an outcry not just among shipping companies but among manufacturers and businesses of many sorts in every corner of the world. Without absolutely certain intelligence—there is a specific device, in a specific box, on a specific ship—the navies simply can't get in the way. This leaves NATO, in its hunt for terrorists, probing through the murk among all the other kinds of ships that could carry equally dangerous cargoes. Intercepts have produced results—most significantly a cargo of centrifuge parts discovered in October 2003 on a German ship bound for Libya, and its now-dismantled nuclear weapons program. But so far no terrorist weapons or devices have been found. And this is hardly a suprise. . . .

## Piracy Demonstrates the Chaos of the Sea

The truth is that naval patrols hardly matter at all. It's not that they are a bad thing, or might not occasionally turn something up, but that they are national tools best applied against nations, and they have little effect against ephemeral gangs on the open ocean. This may be difficult to grasp, because a warship coming over the horizon does instill fear, and the struggle against al Qaeda is too young to make the lack of deterrence clear. But there is longer-standing evidence that can be brought to bear: the growth and persistence of a modern form of extra-national piracy that plagues large swaths of the ocean and has escaped every sea-based effort at control. On a global scale, this sort of piracy is more a nuisance than a threat, and typically it has been overblown in the press, but it is a significant phenomenon nonetheless, because it requires no base and it mimics normal operations where even legitimate ships fly false flags and swap names. Though it is apolitical by nature, it is structurally very similar to the stateless terrorism now faced by government forces.

These pirates are ambitious and well organized, and they should be distinguished from the larger number of petty opportunists whose presence has always afflicted remote ports and coastlines, and whose acts inflate the piracy statistics, but who lack the criminal sophistication to steal more than they can load onto a small boat—some of the ship's stores, or the cash and valuables of the crews on board. Though they may be murderous—and do occasionally strike terror into the Western middle class with their attacks on wandering yachts— these small-time pirates are as insignificant historically as street criminals in dangerous city neighborhoods. A distinction should also be made from the famous "privateers" of old, state-sanctioned agents who were used by governments to attack competing states at a time when merchant sailors resolutely flew their national flags and modern nations were on the rise. The new pirates, by contrast, have emerged on a post-modern ocean, where identities have been mixed and blurred and the rules of nationality have been subverted. Scornful of boundaries, these ambitious pirates are organized into ephemeral multi-ethnic gangs that communicate by satellite and cell phone and are capable of cynically appraising competing jurisdictions and laws. They choose their targets patiently, and then they assemble, strike, and dissipate. They have been known to carry heavy weapons, including shoulder-launched missiles, but they are not determined aggressors, and they will back off from stiff resistance, regroup, and find another way. Usually they succeed with only guns and knives. Box cutters would probably serve them just as well. Their goal in general is to hijack entire ships: they kill or maroon the crews, sell the cargoes, and in the most elaborate schemes turn the hijacked vessels into "phantoms," which, posing as legitimate ships with all the requisite paperwork, pick up new cargoes and disappear.

## Naval Patrols Cannot Impose Order

Owing to the scope of their ambitions, these gangs are responsible for the theft of much of the cargo stolen on the high seas, though they seem to perpetrate relatively few attacks. Given the murkiness of the world they inhabit, the numbers are difficult to calculate. Of 1,228 pirate attacks reported worldwide from 1998 through 2002, about a fourth were on ships under way, and of those about 68 were major, involving gangs of ten pirates or more. It's safe to assume that some in the gangs were repeat offenders. Among them during the five years in question they hijacked perhaps twenty-five large ships. The violence was not evenly distributed throughout the world. Though piracy posed problems off the coasts of South America, Africa, and the Indian subcontinent (and occurred in the very midst of NATO's sea hunt for al Qaeda), roughly two-thirds of the activity was concentrated in just one region—the area of the South China Sea, including the waters of Indonesia and the Philippines. The problem, in other words, would seem finite. Gazing at a map from the confines of land, one might think that with some sea and air patrols, and maybe the "expanded authority" to perform intercepts at sea, order could be imposed. But that authority already exists, and those patrols are being run, and the numbers have only wavered, and order has not come.

# 14

# The Threat of Maritime Terrorism and Piracy Is Exaggerated

*Sam Bateman*

*Sam Bateman is a Professorial Research Fellow at the Centre for Maritime Policy, University of Wollongong, Australia, and a Senior Fellow and Adviser to the Maritime Security Programme at the Institute of Defence and Strategic Studies (IDSS) in Singapore.*

*After September 11, 2001, worries about maritime terrorism escalated. Doomsday scenarios of catastrophic terrorist attacks by water have been discussed and taken seriously. Similarly, some have warned of the threat that increased piracy may lead to terrorist attacks. In fact, however, there has been little evidence that terrorists are focused on or have the capability to launch a major maritime attack. Nor is there good evidence that terrorists and pirates are closely allied, or even that piracy is increasing. Therefore, massive spending and burdensome security measures need to be reevaluated in light of the low likelihood of attacks and the importance of other priorities.*

About 90 percent of the world's trade by volume moves by sea and this volume may double over the next fifteen years. Seaborne trade is potentially vulnerable to terrorist attack due to the quantity of cargo involved, its diverse and large international labor force, difficulties of enforcement both

Sam Bateman, *Violence at Sea: Piracy in the Age of Global Terrorism*. Andover, Hampshire: United Kingdom, Routledge, Taylor & Francis Group, 2007. Copyright © 2007 Taylor & Francis Group, LLC. Reproduced by permission of the publisher.

in port and at sea, and the poor regulatory environment of international shipping with low levels of accountability, complicated chains of ownership, and a high incidence of fraudulent documentation. Terrorists could potentially exploit these weaknesses to use sea transport for evil purposes, or to launch an attack on shipping and port infrastructure that could cause massive economic disruption.

The need to counter the threat of maritime terrorism has led to fundamental changes in the international maritime security environment. The new countermeasures have imposed large additional costs on the transport system and have required significant effort from both government and industry. However at this stage, the maritime terrorist threat has had no significant impact on the volume or pattern of international trade. We have had stronger than expected economic growth in Asia, and this situation would not have been any different without the terrorist attacks on the World Trade Center in New York on 11 September 2001 (9/11). While the maritime terrorist attacks that have occurred in recent years have been relatively minor in terms of their overall impact, the 9/11 attacks are usually regarded as examples of the extreme events that might be possible, including on maritime targets, and for which countermeasures are required.

This [viewpoint] makes a critical assessment of the new threat of maritime terrorism and the outlook into the near future. This includes consideration of the threat and net impact of piracy worldwide, including the possibility that a high incidence of piracy in a particular area might increase the risk of a maritime terrorist attack. . . .

Based on a proposition that there may have been rather too much emphasis on highly remote and speculative "doomsday" scenarios in assessing the risks of maritime terrorism, this [viewpoint] seeks to provide something of a reality check. It attempts to introduce some balance into consideration of the risks and likelihood of a serious maritime terrorist attack occurring somewhere in the world in the near future. The economic impact of the countermeasures to the threat of maritime terrorism may well have been much larger than that of the 9/11 attacks themselves, although undoubtedly the attribution of costs and benefits from the countermeasures have varied significantly between different countries and industry sectors.

The [viewpoint] concludes with a plea for both balance and equity in managing the threat of terrorism. Any one interest group, be it a particular country, group of countries, or a particular industry sector, such as the ship owners, marine insurers, or providers of security equipment or services, should not be in a position from which they can "beat up" a threat and exploit the current situation to their own advantage. Unfortunately, developments in maritime security in recent years provide some examples of this occurring. Horrific scenarios of maritime terrorist attacks that would previously have been dismissed as fantasy have been presented as real and present dangers.

---

*Assessments of the threat of maritime terrorism must be rational and represent a reasonable balance between ... likelihood ... and the costs of providing adequate security.*

---

## Fear of Terrorism at Sea Has Outpaced Reality

Several bestsellers have been written around the threat of maritime terrorism. These usually describe the seizure of an oil tanker or other ship by terrorists who threaten to cause massive nuclear or oil pollution by sinking the vessel unless their demands are met. In 1980 Frederick Forsyth published his novel, *The Devil's Alternative*, in which terrorists hijack an ultralarge crude carrier (ULCC), the *Freya*, a gigantic vessel of fictitious proportions (515 meters long and 90 meters wide), carrying one million tons of crude oil. They threaten to blow the ship up, causing massive pollution of the North Sea, unless colleagues held in a German jail are released.

It may only be a coincidence, but Frederick Forsyth is a shareholder of Aegis Defence Services (ADS), the U.K. company that has made some of the more extreme assessments of the risks of maritime terrorism in recent years. A study published by ADS in October 2003 identified what it said were several new and disturbing developments in maritime terrorism in Southeast Asia, including the assessment that an attack on the chemical tanker *Dewi Madrim* in March 2003 had been a case of terrorists learning to drive a ship. However, the International Maritime Bureau (IMB) stated that its Piracy Reporting Centre (PRC) in Kuala Lumpur had received confirmation from the owners of the ship that the attack was not as described by Aegis. In another somewhat extreme prediction, the intelligence director of ADS claimed in December 2004 that al-Qaeda was likely to launch a spectacular maritime attack during the year 2005.

Despite fictional accounts of maritime terrorism, reality is somewhat different and there have been relatively few confirmed acts of maritime terrorism. Passenger ships and ferries have been preferred targets. The sinking of *Superferry 14* in February 2004 near Manila in the Philippines has been the most serious act of maritime terrorism so far in terms of loss of life with 116 people killed. However, the attacks on the *USS Cole* in Aden in October 2000 [in which the destroyer was struck by a suicide bomber] and on the French tanker *Limburg* off Yemen in October 2002 [in which the oil tanker hit an explosive dinghy] usually attract the most attention in writings on maritime terrorism because they were initiated by al-Qaeda and occurred in the context of 9/11. The numerous maritime terrorist attacks by the "Sea Tigers" of the Liberation Tigers of Tamil Eelam (LTTE) on both merchant ships and Sri

Lankan warships are also often cited as examples of what might be possible, including the assessment that al-Qaeda has benefited from the technologies and techniques of the LTTE.

It is not too difficult to conjure up "doomsday" scenarios for a maritime terrorist attack. A ship carrying a highly dangerous cargo could be hijacked and used as a floating bomb to destroy a port and cause large loss of human life, or a shipping container or a ship itself could be used to import a nuclear bomb or other weapons of mass destruction (WMDs). These are very low-probability, high-consequence scenarios that can lead to some lack of balance in decision making both by governments and the business sector. Assessments of the threat of maritime terrorism must be rational and represent a reasonable balance between the likelihood of an attack occurring and the costs of providing adequate security against such an attack. The assessments depend on a multitude of factors, especially the capabilities and intentions of prospective maritime terrorists, the vulnerability of particular targets, and the consequences of an attack, should one occur.

## Maritime Targets Are Not Attractive to Terrorists

The main maritime terrorist threat is usually seen as coming from al-Qaeda and its associated groups in Southeast Asia, particularly Jemaah Islamiyah (JI), and the Abu Sayyaf Group (ASG). These groups have training camps in the southern Philippines where they train together and share expertise. Members of these groups routinely move between Sabah (Indonesian Borneo) and these camps by speedboat, local craft, and ferries. The ASG in the Philippines has already shown that it can attack ships, having claimed responsibility for the *Superferry 14* attack, and more recently has been blamed for the bomb attack on the ferry *Dona Ramona* in August 2005 as the ship was about to depart from the port of Zamboanga [in the Philippines]. These attacks show that ferries, and potentially cruise liners, are vulnerable to attack. With passenger ships and ferries, it is not so much the bomb that does the damage but rather the fire and panic that might follow an explosion with so many people in a relatively confined area. Threats have been made on ships passing through the Strait of Gibraltar, as well as U.S. Naval ships and facilities in Singapore. In March 2004, Philippine military sources were quoted as saying that the ASG was training with JI to prepare for possible seaborne and underwater attacks outside the Philippines.

---

*The potential list of targets for a terrorist is limitless, but maritime targets may not figure prominently on it.*

---

Terrorism is not just about killing people. An attack that caused maximum disruption to a country's economy or transportation system might be as attractive as an attack that led to major loss of life but did not directly cause disruption. Al-Qaeda has stated that it might attack vital economic centers and strategic enterprises of the "Jewish-Christian alliance," including operations on land, at sea, and in the air. In August 2005, a French terrorism expert warned that Singapore, Tokyo, and Sydney could be targets of an al-Qaeda strike at a major financial center.

In relative terms, maritime targets may be less attractive than land or air targets. Ships at sea are difficult targets, and an attack on port infrastructure may have rather less impact than an attack on a major building or facility (such as a mass transportation system) that has both high economic and iconic value. Unless a ship itself was used as a bomb or as a means of introducing a WMD, a maritime terrorist attack may not cause large loss of life. The destruction of a port facility would have significant economic impact but might not figure prominently in the public consciousness. The potential list of targets for a terrorist is limitless, but maritime targets may not figure prominently on it. The preferred targets for terrorists are likely to remain on land where, as shown by the attacks on mass urban transport in London and Madrid, success is more readily assured.

## Claims of Increasing Piracy May Be Overstated

The incidence of piracy and armed robbery against ships in some parts of the world has led to perceptions of higher risks of terrorist attack in those waters. The number of acts of piracy and armed robbery against ships (actual and attempted) worldwide reported by the IMB in 2004 was 325, a decrease of 120 (27.0 percent) over 2003. By far the greatest concentration of these incidents was in Southeast Asia (156 incidents; 48.0 percent of total attacks worldwide), with 93 of these occurring in Indonesian waters, 9 in Malaysian waters, and 37 in the Malacca Straits. Other concentrations of attacks were in Indian and Bangladeshi waters with 32 reported attacks (9.8 percent), and West Africa with 52 attacks (16.0 percent) mostly off the coast of Nigeria. The annual report of the IMB for 2004 also drew attention to the trend towards greater violence in the attacks, and to an increase in the number of crew killed in attacks from 21 in 2003 to 30 in 2004. Hijacking of small vessels, such as tugs and fishing boats, with their crews held for ransom was also a new and developing phenomenon in some areas around the world.

Some reservations should be noted about the IMB statistics. On the one hand, there could be some underreporting of piratical acts. Both the IMB and the IMO [International Maritime Organization] have noted the reluctance by some ship masters and ship owners to report incidents due to concern that any investigation will disrupt the ship's schedule, the adverse publicity possibly involved, and the possibility that insurance premiums may increase. But on the other hand, over reporting of the number of incidents is also possible. Many of the incidents are really just petty theft (of small items such as paint, mooring ropes, or outboard motors), or occur when a ship is alongside in port or at anchor. . . .

---

*The potential for cooperation between pirates and terrorists has probably been overstated.*

---

The IMB attack statistics often vary widely from one year to the next both in aggregate terms and in particular features of the attacks. Short-term trends are often quoted as support for assessments of increasing violence or incidence of attacks, whereas longer-term trends may give a different picture. For example, the maximum number of total attacks worldwide has generally tended downwards from the total number of attacks worldwide of 469 in 2000. Similarly, while the number of seafarers killed in 2004 (32) was higher than in 2003 (21), greater numbers were in fact killed in earlier years for which data is available: 1998 (78 killed), 2000 (72), and 1997 (51).

Aggregate figures also obscure trends with different types of ship. The current categorization of attacks by vessel type used by the IMB is unsatisfactory for making proper assessments of the risks of piracy to different types of ship. The IMB currently uses 37 different ship types in its database, but most of these do not lend themselves to valid threat assessments (e.g. cable layer, storage ship, and dredger), as very few attacks have occurred in each of these categories over the last decade. On the other hand, some major categories (e.g. container ship, bulk carrier, and tanker) conflate many ships of vastly different size and purpose. These categories record many attacks, but the large figures can distort the picture. For example, smaller, feeder container ships and product tankers on local voyages are much more vulnerable than larger vessels. This can give the impression that "mainline" container vessels and large tankers on international voyages through the Malacca and Singapore straits between Europe or the Middle East and East Asia are being attacked when in fact, they are not.

## Pirates and Terrorists Are Not Likely Allies

The potential for cooperation between pirates and terrorists has probably been overstated. Piracy and maritime terrorism are closely related activities involving "armed violence at sea which is not a lawful act of war." But a distinction exists between the two acts: piracy is conducted for private ends while terrorism has political motives. In assessments of the risk of maritime terrorism, pirates have been seen as having skills and expertise that might be attractive to a terrorist group, but these are not so specialized that they are not readily available. Former naval personnel and fishermen, as well as the multitude of people throughout Asia that have some experience as commercial seafarers, all offer a basis of knowledge that could be of use to a terrorist group. The many terrorist attacks by the Sri Lankan Tamil Tigers on merchant ships and Sri Lankan warships were largely possible because many Tamil Tigers were formerly fishermen.

In June 2005, the London insurance market's Joint War Committee (JWC) declared the Malacca and Singapore straits a "war risk zone." This was on the basis of assessments by ADS that the levels of piracy in the straits were increasing and the pirates were making greater use of small arms and light weapons. ADS also suggested that there were potential links between the incidence of piracy and the risk of terrorism due to the increasing sophistication of weaponry and techniques being used by pirates that made them largely indistinguishable from those of terrorists. This latter assessment has been criticized as there is little or no real evidence to suggest that pirates are forming links with international or regional groups in order to carry out a devastating maritime attack. The increasing use of small arms and light weapons by the pirates is symptomatic of the more general problem associated with the ready availability of these weapons around the world.

For the reasons outlined above, the key assessments by ADS are questionable. Rather than the situation deteriorating in recent years, it could well have improved due to the greater effort by the littoral [coastal] states to ensure the security of shipping in the straits. Despite this, the JWC declaration has justified insurers raising premiums for ships transiting the straits. Both international ship-owning associations and the littoral states concerned have protested the declaration, but the JWC has stuck by its decision, declaring that the Malacca Straits would remain on the "war risk zone" list until "it was clear that the measures planned by governments and other agencies in the area had been implemented and were effective." . . .

## Anti-Terrorism Measures Are Poorly Thought Out

The maritime transportation industry has been greatly affected by the threat of maritime terrorism. It now has a vastly different regulatory environment from the one that prevailed prior to 9/11. However, for the reasons discussed in this [viewpoint] there must be some reservations about the credibility of the threat and the cost benefits of the new countermeasures. We have had a plethora of assertions about the risks and outcomes of a catastrophic maritime terrorist attack, including assessments of a nexus between piracy and maritime terrorism. To some extent, these have distorted perspectives of the probability of a major attack in the future. The maritime terrorist incidents that have occurred have had miniscule impact on the free movement of shipping and seaborne trade in comparison with the massive costs of implementing the new countermeasures.

It is yet to be seen how effective the new measures will be, or indeed how enduring they might be in an international industry that has been characterized by double standards and regulation avoidance. It is essential that a proper balance is maintained between security on the one hand and the free movement of trade on the other. The basic question is one of "how much security is enough?" All the new measures for maritime security imply extra costs for ship owners, port operators, and shippers, including potential delays in the handling of cargo. Additional barriers to competition are involved and some ports, especially ones in developing countries, face difficulties due to their lack of capacity to introduce such measures. There is a real concern over whether all the measures being introduced are appropriate to the threat, as well as a perception that many of the measures only serve the national interests of the United States and other major Western countries.

So far, the approach to countering the threat of maritime terrorism has been a generalized one, with all ships and ports being required to meet new international standards. In the United States for example, the Department of Homeland Security has been criticized for spending millions of dollars on port security without sufficiently focusing on those that are most vulnerable. There would appear to be a need now to modify this approach somewhat by concentrating on key vulnerabilities, including the security of the full supply chain and the identification of ships, port facilities, and cargoes that pose a greater risk. For example, a petrochemical port facility located in a built-up area is clearly much more vulnerable than a bulk ore or grain loading facility in a remote area. Probably too much emphasis has been given to "worst case" scenarios. Despite the huge costs of such a scenario happening, the costs of ensuring against such scenarios are proving to be equally massive. In the interests of responsible public expenditure and avoidance of unreasonable burdens on the private sector, new security measures should be subject to rigorous analysis and testing against realistic and commonsense risk assessments.

The main challenge is how to enhance transportation security without compromising on efficiency and adding to costs. But others include building the capacity of individual countries to manage the risks, achieving some form of standardization across individual ports, ensuring the security of data, achieving a fair distribution of the relevant costs, and sustaining just-in-time (JIT) business practices. As the Secretary General of the International Chamber of Shipping has noted, "It is not far fetched to say that trade . . . is now under threat, not just from terrorism itself but also from the measures that might be taken to combat it."

The countermeasures to the threat of maritime terrorism have imposed major additional costs on ship owners, ports, and shippers. They are also imposing delays on port operations and slowing down the process of international trade. Ports are imposing significant extra charges to cover the costs of additional security, insurance companies have increased security premiums, and providers of security services and equipment are doing good business. Furthermore, the new focus on maritime security has led to an environment of increased naval and military spending generally. When developing countries should be pursuing programs that will drive down poverty and social unrest and thus remove root causes of piracy and terrorism, they are being pressed to improve their capacity to protect their domestic supply chain and to provide maritime security in their adjacent waters.

It is time now for a reality check and to consider the broader maritime strategic and security environment rather than remaining fixated on the threat of maritime terrorism. Problems such as the root causes of piracy and terrorism and the ready availability of small arms around the world must be addressed. There must also be some limit to the current booming levels of naval arms spending in parts of the world. This spending has significant opportunity costs, particularly with regard to the provision of resources to address poverty and injustice. Meanwhile, the international community seems to be giving lower priority and fewer resources to measures to protect and preserve the marine environment and to conserve its biodiversity, despite the established importance of the health of the oceans to the future of the world.

# Organizations to Contact

*The editors have compiled the following list of organizations concerned with the issues debated in this book. The descriptions are derived from materials provided by the organizations. All have publications or information available for interested readers. The list was compiled on the date of publication of the present volume; the information provided here may change. Be aware that many organizations take several weeks or longer to respond to inquiries, so allow as much time as possible.*

**The Atlantic Council of the United States**
1101 15th Street NW, 11th Floor
Washington, DC   20005
(202) 463-7226 • fax: (202) 463-7241
E-mail: info@acus.org
Web site: www.acus.org

The Atlantic Council is a nonpartisan network of leaders devoted to stimulating dialogue about critical international issues affecting the Atlantic community. The council conducts educational and exchange programs focused on American, Asian, European, and NATO issues. Its Web site includes numerous reports and publications on many international issues, including maritime piracy.

**The Brookings Institution**
1775 Massachusetts Ave. NW, Washington, DC   20036-2188
(202) 797-6000
Web site: www.brookings.edu

The institution, founded in 1927, is a liberal think tank that conducts research and education in foreign policy, economics, government, and the social sciences. It publishes the twice-yearly *Brookings Papers on Economic Activity* and various books, including *The Search for Al Qaeda*.

## Center for Arms Control and Non-Proliferation

322 4th Street NE, Washington, DC   20002
(202) 546-0795 • fax: (202) 546-5142
Web site: www.armscontrolcenter.org

The Center for Arms Control and Non-Proliferation is a non-profit, nonpartisan policy organization that is dedicated to enhancing international peace and security and protecting American people from the threat of weapons of mass destruction. The center seeks to reduce and ultimately eliminate nuclear weapons and halt the spread of all weapons of mass destruction. Staff at the organization provides commentary and analysis published in newspapers and journals throughout the world.

## Council on Foreign Relations

58 E. 68th Street, New York, NY   10021
(212) 434-9400 • fax: (212) 434-9800
Web site: www.cfr.org

The council is a group of individuals with specialized knowledge of foreign affairs. It was formed to study the international aspects of American political and economic policies and problems. It publishes the renowned journal *Foreign Affairs* six times a year.

## Forcign Policy Association

470 Park Ave. South, New York, NY   10016
Ph:(212) 481-8100 • fax: (212) 481-9275
E-mail: info@fpa.org
Web site: www.fpa.org

The association is an educational organization that provides nonpartisan information to help citizens participate in foreign policy decisions. It publishes irregularly the *Headline Series* and the annual *Great Decisions*.

## Institute of Southeast Asian Studies (ISEAS)

30 Heng Mui Keng Terrace, Pasir Panjang   119614
   Singapore
(65) 6778 0955 • fax: (65) 6778 1735
E-mail: admin@iseas.edu.org
Web site: www.iseas.edu.sg

ISEAS is a regional research center dedicated to the study of sociopolitical, security, and economic trends and developments in Southeast Asia. It conducts research programs, holds conferences, and provides a range of research support facilities. It is home to ISEAS Publications, which has published important scholarly books on piracy in Indonesia and the Malacca Strait. It also publishes journals, annuals, and a newsletter.

## International Chamber of Commerce (ICC)
## Commercial Crime Services

Cinnabar Wharf, 26 Wapping High Street
London   E1W 1NG
   UK
44 (0) 20 7423 6960 • fax: 44 (0) 20 7423 6961
E-mail: ccs@icc-ccs.org
Web site: www.icc-ccs.org

ICC Commercial Crime Services is the anti-crime arm of the International Chamber of Commerce. It includes the International Maritime Bureau (IMB), which is a nonprofit organization established to work against maritime crime. The IMB identifies and investigates maritime fraud and crime, runs courses and training programs, and provides information for members. It also maintains the IMB Piracy Reporting Centre, which issues to shipping warnings about piracy hot spots and provides updated online information about recent pirate activity.

## International Maritime Organization (IMO)

Offices of the Secretariat, 4 Albert Embankment
London   SE1 7SR
  UK
44 (0) 20 7735 7611 • fax: 44 (0) 20 7587 3210
E-mail: rcoenen@imo.org
Web site: www.imo.org

IMO is an agency of the United Nations charged with developing and maintaining a comprehensive regulatory framework for shipping. IMO produces and updates conventions on shipping. The organization produces an extensive range of publications in numerous languages about shipping regulations and other maritime matters.

## Maritime Law Association of the United States (MLA)

Warren J. Marwedel, president;
Marwedel, Minichello & Reeb PC, Chicago, IL   60606
(312) 902-1600, ext. 5054 • fax: (312) 902-9900
E-mail: wmarwedel@mmr-law.com
Web site: www.mlaus.org

The MLA is an organization dedicated to reforming and unifying U.S. and international maritime law. The MLA formulates policy recommendations and hosts seminars and panel discussions. The organization's proceedings, reports, and other publications are available through its Web site.

## RAND Corporation

1776 Main Street, Santa Monica, CA   90401-3208
Tel: (877) 584-8642; (310) 393-0411 • fax: (310) 393-4818
E-mail: order@rand.org
Web site: www.rand.org

The RAND Corporation is a nonprofit organization dedicated to improving policy through research and analysis. RAND research is commissioned by both public and private groups. RAND has an extensive library of publications and reports, including a number on piracy, available in print or by download from its Web site.

## United Nations Division for Ocean Affairs and the Law of the Sea (UN DOALOS)

Office of Legal Affairs, Room DC2-0450, United Nations
New York, NY 10017
(212) 963-3962 • fax: (212) 963-5847
E-mail: doalos@un.org
Web site: www.un.org/depts/los/index.htm

The UN Division for Ocean Affairs provides information and advice to states and individuals about the international law of the sea. It maintains an information system and reference library and runs educational and training programs. DOALOS prepares documents and pamphlets dealing with ocean affairs and the law of the sea.

## United States Coast Guard (USCG)

Coast Guard Headquarters, Commandant, U.S. Coast Guard
2100 Second Street SW, Washington, DC 20593
Web site: www.uscg.mil

USCG is a military branch of the United States involved in maritime law, mariner assistance, and the protection of U.S. economic and security interests in international and American waterways. The Coast Guard produces a number of publications, including *Proceedings of the Marine Safety & Security Council: The Coast Guard Journal of Safety at Sea.*

## United States Department of Homeland Security (DHS)

U.S. Department of Homeland Security
Washington, DC 20528
(202) 282-8000
Web site: www.dhs.gov

DHS's mission is to secure the United States against all hazards and disasters, with a particular focus on terrorism prevention. DHS is responsible for border control and oversees the Coast Guard, among many other duties. Plans, reports, brochures, and other publications are available on its Web site.

## Woodrow Wilson International Center for Scholars

Ronald Reagan Building and International Trade Center
One Woodrow Wilson Plaza, Washington, DC 20004-3027
(202) 691-4000
Web site: www.wilsoncenter.org

The Wilson Center is a nonpartisan institute for advanced study and a neutral forum for open, serious, and informed dialogue. It brings preeminent thinkers to Washington for extended periods of time to interact with policymakers. It produces numerous publications, including the *Wilson Quarterly*.

# Bibliography

## Books

Sam Bateman

*Security and International Politics in the South China Sea: Towards a Cooperative Management Regime.* New York, NY: Routledge, 2008.

John S. Burnett

*Dangerous Waters: Modern Piracy and Terror on the High Seas.* London: Penguin Books, Ltd., 2002.

Peter Chalk

*The Maritime Dimension of International Security: Terrorism, Piracy, and Challenges for the United States.* Santa Monica, CA: RAND Corporation, 2008.

David Cordingly

*Under the Black Flag: The Romance and the Reality of Life Among the Pirates.* Orlando, FL: Harcourt, 1995.

Gregory Fremont-Barnes

*Wars of the Barbary Pirates: To the Shores of Tripoli: The Birth of the U.S. Navy and Marines.* New York, NY: Osprey Publishing, 2006.

Graham Gerard Ong-Webb

*Piracy, Maritime Terrorism and Securing the Malacca Straits.* Singapore: ISEAS Publications, 2006.

Michael D. Greenberg

*Maritime Terrorism: Risk and Liability.* Santa Monica, CA: RAND Corporation, 2006.

Rupert Herbert-Burns, Sam Bateman, Peter Lehr, eds.

*Lloyd's MIU Handbook of Maritime Security.* Boca Raton, FL: Auerbach Publications, 2009.

Klaus Hympendahl

*Pirates Aboard! Forty Cases of Piracy Today and What Bluewater Cruisers Can Do About It.* Dobbs Ferry, NY: Sheridan House, 2003.

Angus Konstam

*Piracy: The Complete History.* New York, NY: Osprey Publishing, 2008.

Max Lane

*Unfinished Nation: Indonesia Before and After Suharto.* Brooklyn, NY: Verso, 2008.

Benerson Little

*The Sea Rover's Practice: Pirate Tactics and Techniques, 1630–1730.* Dulles, VA: Potomac Books, Inc., 2005.

Benerson Little

*The Buccaneer's Realm: Pirate Life on the Spanish Main, 1674–1688.* Dulles, VA: Potomac Books, Inc., 2007.

Ken Menkhaus

*Somalia: State Collapse and the Threat of Terrorism.* New York, NY: Oxford University Press, 2004.

Martin N. Murphy

*Small Boats, Weak States, Dirty Money: Piracy and Maritime Terrorism in the Modern World.* New York, NY: Columbia University Press, 2009.

Richard Lloyd Parry

*In the Time of Madness: Indonesia on the Edge of Chaos.* London: Random House, 2005.

Michael
Richardson
*A Time Bomb for Global Trade:
Maritime-related Terrorism in the Age
of Weapons of Mass Destruction.*
Singapore: ISEAS Publications, 2004.

Shaul Shay
*Somalia Between Jihad and
Restoration.* Piscataway, NJ:
Transaction Publishers, 2008.

Frank Sherry
*Raiders and Rebels: A History of the
Golden Age of Piracy.* New York, NY:
Harper Perennial, 2008.

## Periodicals

Arthur Bowring
"The Price of Piracy," *The Wall Street
Journal Asia*, November 25, 2008.

John S. Burnett
"The Next 9/11 Could Happen at
Sea," *The New York Times*, February
22, 2005.

Kristen Chick
"Piracy 'Surge' off Somali Coast,"
*Christian Science Monitor*, April 7,
2009.

Andrew
Cockburn
"Somalia: A Failed State?" *National
Geographic*, July 2002.

*The Economist*
"The Indonesian Surprise," April 2,
2009.

*The Economist*
"Piracy and Much Worse," October 2,
2008.

*The Economist*
"The Threat of Maritime Terrorism,"
June 30, 2004.

Robert Farley — "Somali Piracy Is Everyone's Problem," *The Guardian*, November 20, 2008.

Jeffrey Fleishman — "Egypt Calls Meeting to Discuss Stopping Piracy," *Los Angeles Times*, November 21, 2008.

Jeffrey Gettleman — "Somalia's Pirates Flourish in a Lawless Nation," *The New York Times*, October 31, 2008.

Jeffrey Gettleman — "Somali Pirates Tell Their Side: They Want Only Money," *The New York Times*, September 30, 2008.

Tony Karon with Douglas Waller — "Who's Behind the Dubai Company in U.S. Harbors?" *Time Magazine*, February 20, 2006.

Alex Kingsbury — "Piracy: A $50 Million Business and Counting," *U.S. News & World Report*, January 13, 2009.

James Kraska and Brian Wilson — "Fighting Piracy," *Armed Forces Journal*, February 2009.

Samantha Levine — "Shoring up the Nation's Ports," *U.S. News & World Report*, January 4, 2004.

Kang Siew Li — "Straits of Malacca Seeing Drop in Piracy Attacks," *Business Times*, January 19, 2009.

Gal Luft and Anne Korin — "Terrorism Goes to Sea," *Foreign Affairs*, November/December 2004.

| | |
|---|---|
| *The Maritime Executive* | "INTERMANAGER Condemns Lack of Action on Piracy," October 2, 2008. |
| Kelly McEvers | "How (Not) To Find a Pirate in the Strait of Malacca," *Slate.com*, December 1, 2008. |
| Alex Perry | "A Brief Trip to Pirate Island," *National Geographic Adventure*, February 2009. |
| Derek S. Reveron | "Think Again: Pirates," *Foreign Policy Online*, January 2009. |
| Bruno Shiemsky | "Piracy's Rising Tide—Somali Piracy Develops and Diversifies," *Jane's Security News*, January 20, 2009. |
| D.J. Siegelbaum | "Piracy Sparks High-Tech Defenses," *Time Magazine*, April 18, 2008. |
| Brett Stephens | "Why Don't We Hang Pirates Anymore?" *The Wall Street Journal*, November 25, 2008. |

# Index

## A

Abu Sayyaf Group (ASG), 30, 99–100

Accompanying Sea Security Teams (ASSeT) of Singapore, 15

Adams, Cecil, 8

Admiralty courts, 63

Aegis Defence Services (ADS), 98, 103

Afghanistan, 55, 89

Air patrol, 14

Al Qaeda
    al-Shabaab and, 49
    deterrence of, 92
    identification of members, 63
    maritime terrorism and, 42, 44, 85–94
    Nova Spirit and, 89–90
    U.S. invasion of Iraq and, 81

"Al Qaeda Navy," 88

Al-Shabaab, 44, 46, 48, 49

Ali, Sugule, 78

Anarchy, 17

Anti-Piracy Maritime Security Solutions, 45

Antony, A.K., 57, 58

Arabian Sea, 56

Arizona State University, 65

Armed robbery, 12

Autonomous Region of Muslim Mindanao (ARMM), 25

## B

Bahrain, 56

Bangladesh, 101

Barbary corsairs
    diplomatic agreements with, 37–38
    European response to, 38–39
    factors necessary for sustainability of, 39–40
    kidnapping and, 33–34, 36
    popular image, 7
    religious ideology and, 33–37
    slavery and, 35, 37, 38
    suppression of, 39–40, 61
    violence of, 36–37
    *See also* Golden Age of Pirates

Barre, Siad, 50

Barrie, J.M., 7

Bateman, Sam, 95–107

Bin Laden, Osama, 87–88

*Biscaglia* (ship), 45

"Boat people" (Vietnamese), 25

*Booty: Girl Pirates on the High Sea* (Lorimer), 8

Brigands, 62

British Foreign Office, 63

Brunei, 19

*Buccaneer's Realm: Pirate Life on the Spanish Main, 1674–1688* (Little), 80

Bush, George W., 49, 88

## C

Cadmium, 77

Cambodia, 14

Canada, 90

Canary Islands, 36

Casey, Lee A., 60–64

Celebes Sea, 29–30

Chemical tankers, 45
China, 22, 67, 75
Christianity, 33–37
Clan system, 41–42, 47
Coast Guard, 68–70
Combined Task Force 150 (CTF-150), 56
Convention on the Suppression of Unlawful Acts (SUA) of IMO, 18
Cordingly, David, 7
Crews, 22
Cruisers, 68
CTF-150 (Combined Task Force 150), 56

**D**

DD(X), 66
Delaware, 89
Deterrence of piracy, 14
*The Devil's Advocate* (Forsyth), 97–98
*Dewi Madrim* (ship), 98
Diplomatic agreements with pirates, 37–38
*Dona Ramona* (ferry), 99
"Doomsday" scenarios, 96–97, 99
Drugs, 21

**E**

East-West Center in Hawaii, 20
Economics
    class warfare, 82
    costs of terrorism, 87
    economic causes for piracy, 20–26
    effects of piracy, 11, 18, 45
    fishing industry, 23–24
    globalization, 20
    insurance, 11, 18, 55, 61, 87, 101, 106
    shipping growth and, 22
Egypt, 52, 90–91
England, 36
Environment
    economic growth and, 24
    piracy as cause of environmental disaster, 11–12
    toxic waste dumping in Somali waters, 45, 77–79
Equip Program (U.S. program), 29, 30
Ethiopia, 48
European Union (EU), 56
Extortion, 21
"Eye in the Sky" plan, 14

**F**

*Faina* (ship), 51
Farley, Robert, 65–70
"FIG-7" ships, 69
Fishing industry
    Indonesia and, 23–24
    Philippines and, 23–24
    poaching, 24, 46, 50, 51, 53, 83
    Thailand and, 24
    toxic waste dumping and, 45, 78–79
    Volunteer Coastguard of Somalia and, 78–79
Flags of convenience, 13, 22
Food shipments, 60
Foreign Ministry of Indonesia, 71
Forsyth, Frederick, 97
France, 36, 51, 63, 72, 87, 98
Fraud, 11
Free Aceh Movement (GAM), 73

# G

Gangs, 92–94
Germany, 91
Gladstone, William, 57
Global Train (U.S. program), 29, 30
Globalization, 20
Golden Age of Pirates
    common conception of, 7–9
    dates of, 32
    factors necessary for sustainability of, 33
    legacy of, 42–43
    misrepresentation of piracy, 76
    motivations for piracy, 75
    violence and, 32–33
    *See also* Barbary corsairs
Gortzak, Yoav, 65–70
Goyal, P.K., 54
Gross domestic produce (GDP), 20
Gulf of Aden, 45, 50, 52, 56
Gulf of Oman, 56, 89
Gulf of Thailand, 24

# H

Hari, Johann, 75–79
Hartley, Aidan, 44–49
Hezbollah, 58
Hong Kong, 25, 58
Hot pursuit, 12, 17, 57, 59
Human rights, 63, 89
Human smuggling, 89
Humanitarian aid, 60, 71–72

# I

Iceland, 36
Identification, 22, 23

IMO, Convention on the Suppression of Unlawful Acts (SUA), 18
India
    Indian Navy, 57, 58, 59
    kidnappings of Indian sailors, 58
    piracy and, 101
    shipping insurance and, 55
    Somali pirates and, 56
Indian Ocean, 56
Indian-owned ships, 54
Indonesia
    Al Qaeda and, 99
    defense budget, 31
    fishing industry, 23
    Foreign Ministry, 1
    Free Aceh Movement (GAM), 73
    international aid and, 29
    ISPS Code and, 18
    Joint War Committee (JWC) report and, 18
    maritime crime in, 30, 93–94
    maritime security measures, 11, 13, 16–18, 27–29, 52
    "patrol fatigue" and, 30
    piracy in Indonesian waters, 101
    poverty in, 16
    terrorism in, 30
    unemployment, 25
    U.S. aid and, 29–30
Institute of Defence and Strategic Studies (IDSS) in Singapore, 95
Institute of Southeast Asian Studies, 27
Insurance
    Joint War Committee (JWC) effect on, 18
    piracy acts and increased premiums, 11, 55, 101

piracy reporting and, 101
ransom payments and, 61
security measures and, 106
terrorism and, 87
International Maritime Bureau (IMB), 27, 30, 54, 61, 98, 101
International Maritime Organization (IMO), 101
International Ship and Port Facility Security Code (ISPS Code), 12–13
Iraq, 18, 49
Islam
    Barbary corsairs and, 33–37
    piracy and Islamic law, 47, 48, 49
    piracy funding militant Islam, 46
    Shariah, 63
    Somalia and, 42, 55
Israel, 58
Italiano, Michele Filippo, 90–91
Italy, 77–78, 89

**J**

Jane's Terrorism & Security Monitor, 46
Japan, 14–15, 18
Jefferson, Thomas, 61
Jemaah Islamiyah (JI), 30, 99–100
Joint War Committee (JWC) of Lloyd's Market Association, 17–18, 103
Joint Warfare, 68
Jolo, 25
Jurisdiction, 12, 13, 60–63

**K**

Kenya, 52, 60, 88
Kidnapping, 33–34, 36–37, 46–47
Kurniawan, Rama Anom, 71–74

**L**

Laitin, David, 57
Langewiesche, William, 85–94
*Le Ponant* (ship), 51
Lead, 77
Lebanon, 18, 58
Lehr, Peter, 50–53
Liberation societies for kidnap victims, 37
Liberation Tigers of Tamil Eelam (LTTE), 98–99
Libya, 91
*Limburg* (ship), 87
Lingo, 8
Little, Benerson, 80–84
Littoral Combat Ship (LCS), 65–67
Lloyd's Market Association, 17–18
Lorimer, Sara, 8
Lunsford, Virginia, 32–43

**M**

*Maersk Alabama* (ship), 9
Maersk Sealand, 90
Malacca Strait Patrols (MSPs), 28, 30
Malaysia
    international aid and, 29
    Maritime Enforcement Agency, 15
    maritime security measures, 13, 15, 17, 28

piracy and, 101
Strait of Malacca and, 11, 52
Maldives, 58
Maritime Enforcement Agency of
Malaysia, 15
Maritime terrorism
Al Qaeda and, 42, 44, 85–94
as exaggerated, 95–107
novels about, 97–98
Marxism, 82
Mediterranean Sea, 38
Mercenaries, 82
Mercury, 77
Military courts, 60–64
Morocco, 39
Myanmar, 19

**N**

*Nagasaki Spirit* (ship), 12
Nanyang Technological University
in Singapore, 10
Napoleonic Wars, 67–68
National Volunteer Coast Guard
of Somalia, 51
NATO (North Atlantic Treaty
Organization), 56, 62, 63, 88–89,
91, 93
Naval Reserve Force, 69
Netherlands, 36, 39
*New York Times,* 9
Nigeria, 101
Nova Scotia, 90
Nova Spirit, 89–90
Nuclear waste, 77

**O**

*Ocean Blessing* (ship), 12
Oil prices, 22
Oil spills, 86

Oil tankers, 12, 52, 60, 72, 86–87,
98
Oliver Hazard Perry class frigates,
67, 69
Otterman, Sharon, 9
Ottoman Empire, 34, 35, 40
Ould-Abdallah, Ahmedou, 77–78

**P**

Pai, Nitin, 54–59
Pakistan, 49, 56, 58, 89
Parrots, 7
Passports, 22, 47, 89, 90
"Patrol fatigue," 30
*Peter Pan* (Barrie), 7
Philippines
Al Qaeda and, 99
*Dona Ramona* (ferry), 99
maritime crime in, 30, 93–94
SUA and, 19
*Superferry 14,* 98, 99
terrorism in, 30
unemployment, 25
U.S. aid and, 29
Piracy
as apolitical, 92
as armed robbery, 12
decrease in, 39–40, 61, 101
economic effects of, 11, 45, 55
factors necessary for sustainability of, 33, 39–41
gangs, 92–94
goals, 93
illegal fishing as, 24
motivations for, 46–47, 75,
81–83
pirate lingo, 8
planning piracy, 72–74
poaching and, 24, 46, 50, 51,
53, 83

popular image of, 7
prevalence of, 27–28, 54, 56,
   93, 101–102
punishment and, 36–37
religious ideology and, 33–37
terrorism and, 80–84, 103–104
violence, 8–9, 32–33, 36–37,
   61, 71, 81
*See also* Barbary corsairs
Piracy Reporting Center (PRC), 98
Pirate flag, 7, 8
*Pirates of the Caribbean* (film), 7
Poaching, 24, 46, 50, 51, 53, 83
Portugal, 36, 38
Poverty
   Indonesia and, 16
   piracy as response to, 23–26,
      80, 82, 106
   reduction of, 21
Private security companies, 16–17
Prosecution of pirates
   difficulty of, 62–64
   "hot pursuit" and, 12, 17
   human rights issues, 63
   jurisdiction issues, 12, 13, 17,
      60–63
   military courts, 60–64
Prostitution, 21
Punishment, 36–37
Puntland Intelligence Service
   (PIS), 48

**Q**

Quadrennial Defense Review, 66

**R**

Radar surveillance, 15
Ransoms, 9, 37, 46–48, 61, 101
Red Sea, 36, 56, 59
Rediker, Marcus, 76

Regional Cooperation Agreement
   on Anti-Piracy (ReCAAP), 14–16
Religious ideology, 33–37. *See also*
   specific religions
Resolution 1816 of UN Security
   Council, 57
Revenge, 82
Riau Islands, 28
Rivkin, David B., 60–64
Rizk, Amid Farid, 90–91
*Robinson Crusoe* (Defoe), 8
Romania, 89
Royal Navy (UK), 63, 67–68, 75
Rules of engagement, 59
Russia, 56, 68

**S**

Sadie the Goat, 8
Salafi Islam, 49
*Sara* (ship), 89
Saudi Arabia, 45, 50, 60, 72
*Scoop* (Waugh), 44
Scott, William, 77, 78
*Sea Rover's Practice: Pirate Tactics
   and Techniques, 1630–1730*
   (Little), 80
Sea Tigers of Liberation Tigers of
   Tamil Eelam (LTTE), 98–99
*Seabourn Spirit* (ship), 50
Section 1206 authorization, 29
Security measures
   Accompanying Sea Security
      Teams (ASSeT), 15
   air patrol, 14
   anti-terrorism measures, 104–
      107
   coastal surveillance, 29
   Combined Task Force 150
      (CTF-150), 56

efficiency of shipping and, 106–107
European Union anti-piracy taskforce, 56
Gulf of Aden and, 52–53
Indonesia and, 11, 13, 16–18, 27–29, 52
International Ship and Port Facility Security Code (ISPS Code), 12–13
private security companies, 16–17
radar surveillance, 15
Regional Cooperation Agreement on Anti-Piracy (ReCAAP), 14–16
Somalia pirates and, 55
Southeast Asian nations and, 10–19
Trilateral Coordinated Patrol, 12, 13
U.S. Coast Guard and, 68–70
U.S. Navy and, 65–68
Selkirk, Alexander, 8
September 11 terrorist attacks, 17, 49, 86, 96, 104
Shariah (Islamic law), 63
Singapore
Accompanying Sea Security Teams (ASSeT), 15
maritime security measures, 13
Regional Cooperation Agreement on Anti-Piracy (ReCAAP), 14–15
security improvements, 28–29
Strait of Malacca and, 11, 52
SUA and, 19
terrorist threats and, 100
Singapore Straits, 11–12
*Sirius Star* (ship), 52, 60, 72
Slavery, 35, 37, 38, 61, 77

Smuggling, 25, 86, 89
Somali Marines, 51
Somalia
foreign aid for, 48
government of, 9
humanitarian aid, 60, 71–72
Joint War Committee (JWC) report and, 18
kidnapping crimes and, 28
piracy and, 9, 28
political instability, 45–46, 74, 83
toxic waste dumping in Somali waters, 45, 77–79
Somali pirates
behavior of, 47–58
clan system, 41–42, 47
as Coast Guard, 51–52
factors necessary for sustainability of, 40–41
financial success, 51
fish-poaching in Somali waters, 45–46, 50, 51–53, 78–79, 83
Golden Age of Piracy compared with, 32–43
modus operandi, 52
motivations of, 46–47, 75
National Volunteer Coast Guard of Somalia, 51
overview of, 45–47
ransoms and, 46–48
Somali government support of, 41, 47
Somali Marines, 51
statistics, 54
terrorists compared with, 80–84
Volunteer Coastguard of Somalia, 78
South Carolina, 77
South China Sea, 93–94

Southeast Asian nations
  anarchy and, 17
  anti-piracy efforts, 10–19
  economic crisis, 24–26
  economic progress in, 20–23
  industrialization, 21
  maritime traffic and, 22
  *See also* specific nations
Spain, 36, 38, 51
Special Air Service (UK), 47
Sri Lanka, 58, 98–99
Stanford University, 57
Stevenson, Robert Louis, 7, 8, 9
*Stolt Valor* (ship), 54
Storey, Jan, 27
Stowaways, 90–91
*Straight Dope* (Adams), 8
Strait of Gibraltar, 100
Strait of Makassar, 29
Strait of Malacca
  air patrol over, 14
  coast surveillance, 29
  environmental disaster possibilities and, 12
  Indonesia and, 11
  overview of, 27
  piracy reduction, 28
  pirate attacks in, 9
  risk assessment of, 17–18
  "war risk zone," 103
Strikes, 18
Suicide bombers, 48, 98
Sulu Sea, 30
*Superferry 14,* 98, 99

**T**

Taiwan, 51
Taliban, 63
Tankers
  chemical tankers, 45

oil tankers, 12, 45, 52, 60, 72, 87
Tanzania, 52, 88
Tawi Tawi, 25
Terrorism
  anarchy and, 61
  anti-terrorism measures, 104–107
  impact of maritime terrorism, 104
  Joint War Committee (JWC) and, 18
  novels about, 97–98
  piracy and, 17, 80–84, 103–104
  Somalia crisis and, 46
  Strait of Malacca and, 30
  *See also* Maritime terrorism
Thailand, 14, 24, 25, 52, 90
*The Sullivans* (ship), 87
Tonga, 89
Toxic waste dumping in Somali waters, 45, 77–79
*Treasure Island* (Stevenson), 7
Trilateral Coordinated Patrols, 12, 13
Tripoli, 40
Trott, Nicholas, 62
Tsunami, 13, 77
"Turk's rate" tax, 37
Twenty-foot container equivalents (TEUs), 22

**U**

Ukraine, 60
*Under the Black Flag: The Romance and the Reality of Life Among the Pirates* (Cordingly), 7
United Kingdom, 56

United Nations Convention on the Law of the Sea, 74

United Nations Security Council Resolution 733, 71

United Nations Security Council Resolution 1816, 57, 72, 73, 74

United Nations Security Council Resolution 1838, 72

United States
    anti-piracy aid, 29–30
    CTF-150 and, 56
    Defense Security and Cooperation Agency, 30
    Equip Program, 30
    Global Train program, 29
    Library of Congress, 57

Universal jurisdiction, 62–63

University of Kentucky, 65

University of St. Andrews (Scotland), 10, 50

University of Wollongong (Australia), 95

Unlawful enemy combatants, 62

UPA (United Progressive Alliance), 57

U.S. Coast Guard, 68–70

U.S. Department of Homeland Security, 105

U.S. Navy, 9, 47–48, 56, 65–68, 87, 100

U.S. Navy SEALS, 80

USS *Cole* (ship), 87, 98

**V**

Vietnam, 19, 24

Vietnamese "boat people," 25

Violence
    IMB reporting and, 101
    piracy and, 8–9, 32–33, 36–37, 61, 71, 81, 103–104
    terrorism and, 80

Volunteer Coastguard of Somalia, 78

**W**

WardheerNews, 78

Waugh, Evelyn, 44

Weapons, 60, 91, 93, 99, 103–107. *See also* Violence

Weinberger, Seth, 55

Welfare programs, 16

*William of All Nations* (Rediker), 76

World Food Programme, 55, 78

**Y**

Yemen, 18, 87, 98

Young, Adam J., 20–26

Yudhoyono, Susilo Bambang, 28

Yusuf, Abdullahi, 47, 48